I0475957

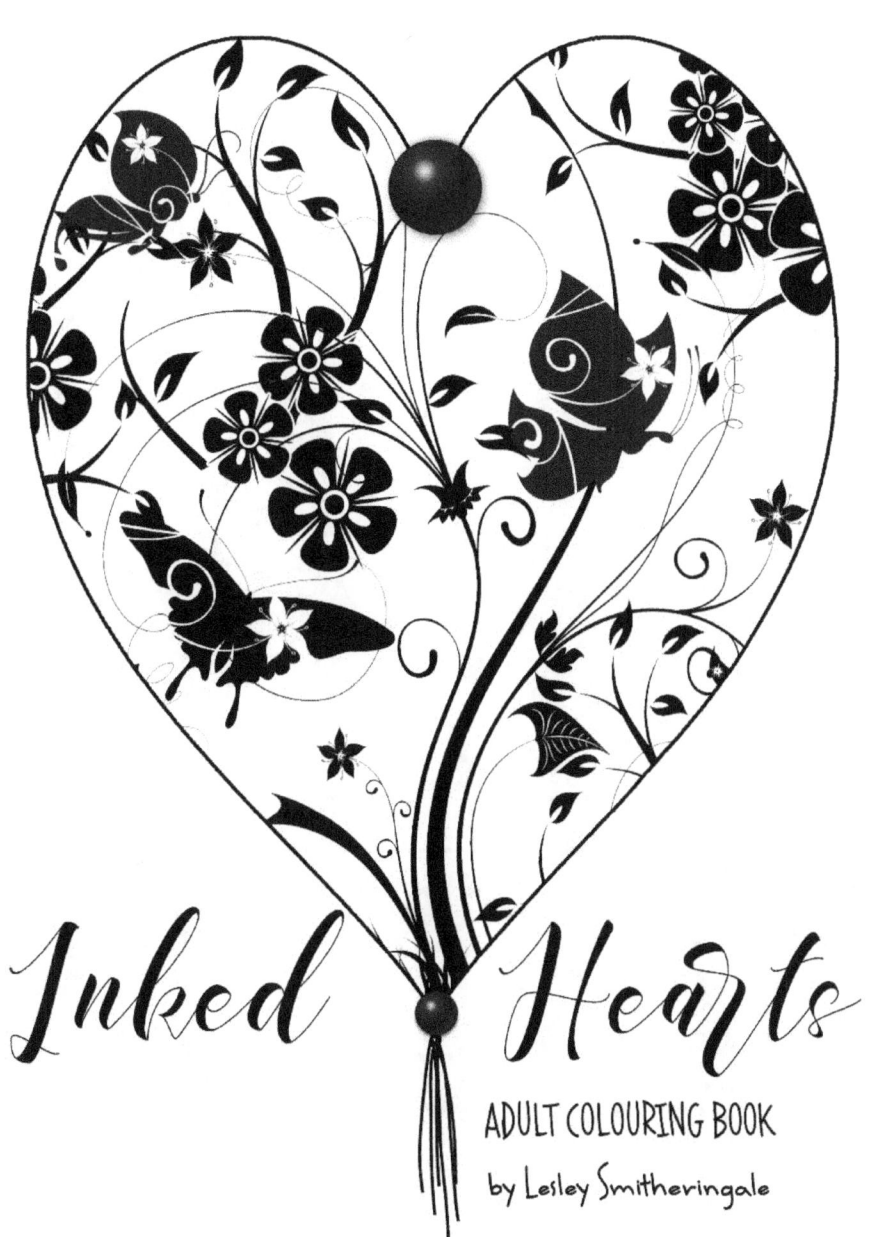

Inked Hearts

ADULT COLOURING BOOK

by Lesley Smitheringale

Inked Hearts

ADULT COLOURING BOOK

by Lesley Smitheringale

About the Artist

Lesley lives and works in her home studio in the Redlands area of Queensland, Australia. She was born in Glasgow, Scotland where she obtained a BA with Honours in Design at Glasgow School of Art. She then did further training to become an art teacher and after teaching for twenty years to Middle and High School students, Lesley took the plunge and decided to work for herself. She currently teaches extra-curricular art to children, produces her own artwork, hand-made gifts, illustrates and self-publishes art & craft books.

Keep up-to-date

If you love to colour and tangle, Lesley also runs a website and online Shop at Colouring and Tangling where she offers inspiration, tips & techniques, video instruction and a large range of products such as books, printable pdfs, calendars, cards, bookmarks, artist prints and giftware for colourists and lovers of zentangle-inspired art.
She also hosts a Facebook Group called Lesley Smitheringale's Art Colouring Group which customers and fans of her work can join, offering you the opportunity to showcase your colourings from any of Lesley's books and resources and meet a creative, virtual community.

http://www.colouringandtangling.com
https://www.facebook.com/groups/LesleySmitheringaleArtColouring/
https://www.etsy.com/shop/ColouringandTangling

How to Assemble the Corner Heart Bookmarks

www.colouringandtangling.com

Instructions:

1. Print, colour then cut out hearts.
2. Fold Hearts in half and along edge of tab
3. Glue top of tab, tuck it <u>inside</u> the two folded heart shapes, press and leave to dry.
4. Slide over corner of page in book
5. To make the bookmarks more durable spray them with a varnish or rub on some pva glue or mod podge which will make them glossy, and water resistant.

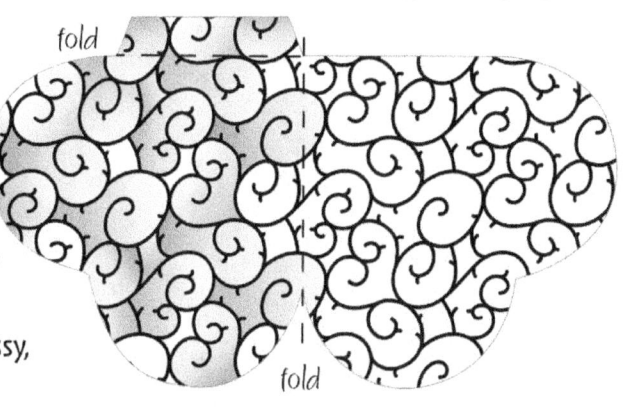

fold

fold

Watch the Video

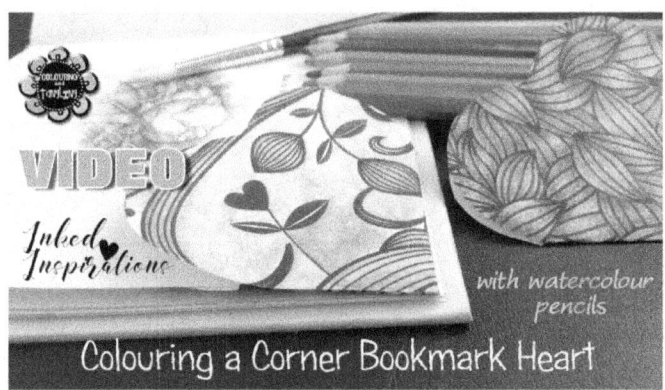

VIDEO

Inked Inspirations

with watercolour pencils

Colouring a Corner Bookmark Heart

I show you how I coloured a corner bookmark heart using watercolour pencils and then assembled it in this video at https://youtu.be/2OJzj8sbjXY

The finished Hanging

How to Assemble the CD Hanging

This is such an inexpensive way to recycle all of those old CD Roms you have lying around the house. Using the templates, colour them, cut them out, glue them onto the front and back of a CD or DVD rom. Drill a hole, thread through some pretty beads and make a loop at the end of your hanging.

See the step-by-step stages in a blog post I wrote on my website at

http://www.colouringandtangling.com/valentines-day/diy-valentine-gift-using-colouring-pages/

This Book Belongs to

_____

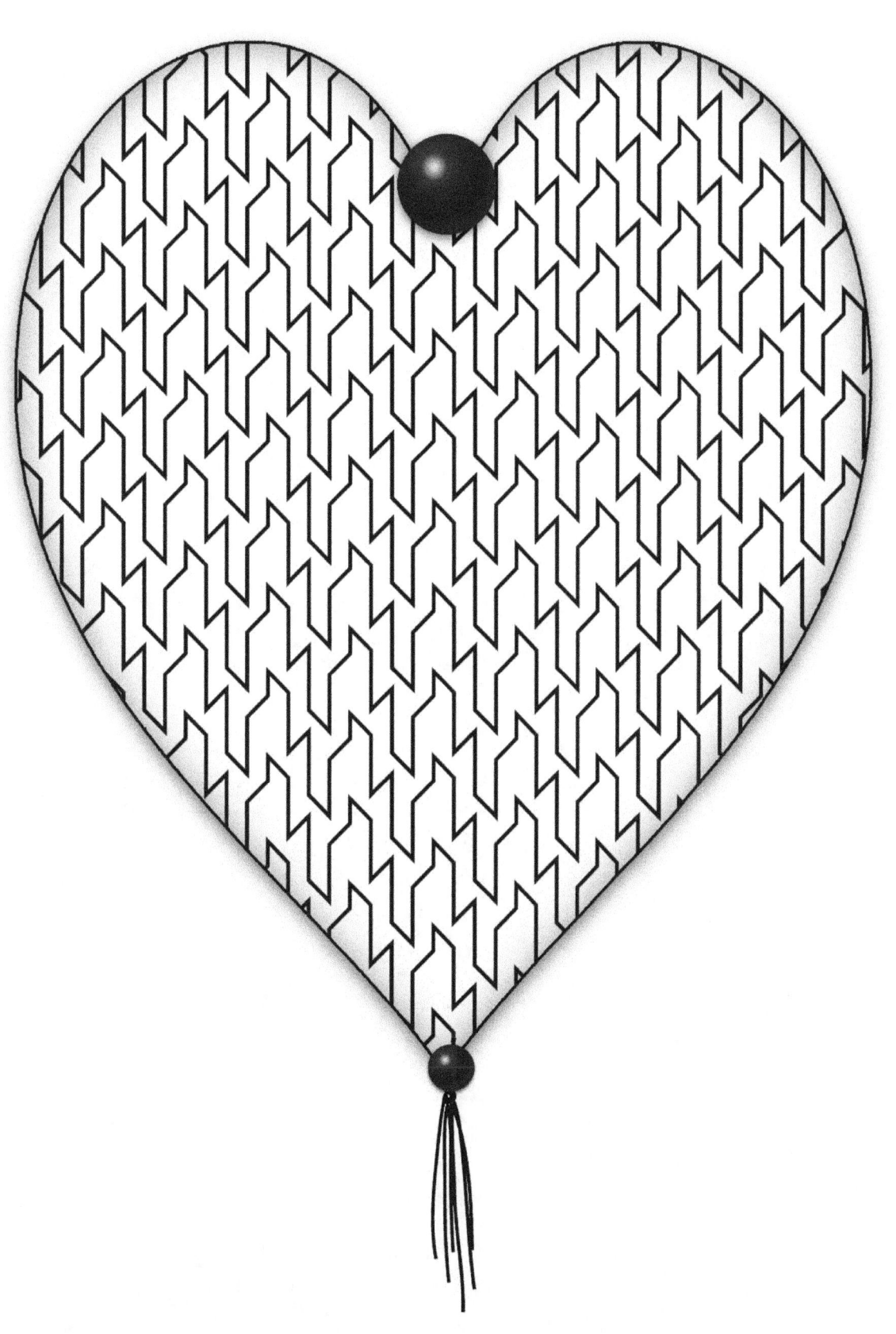

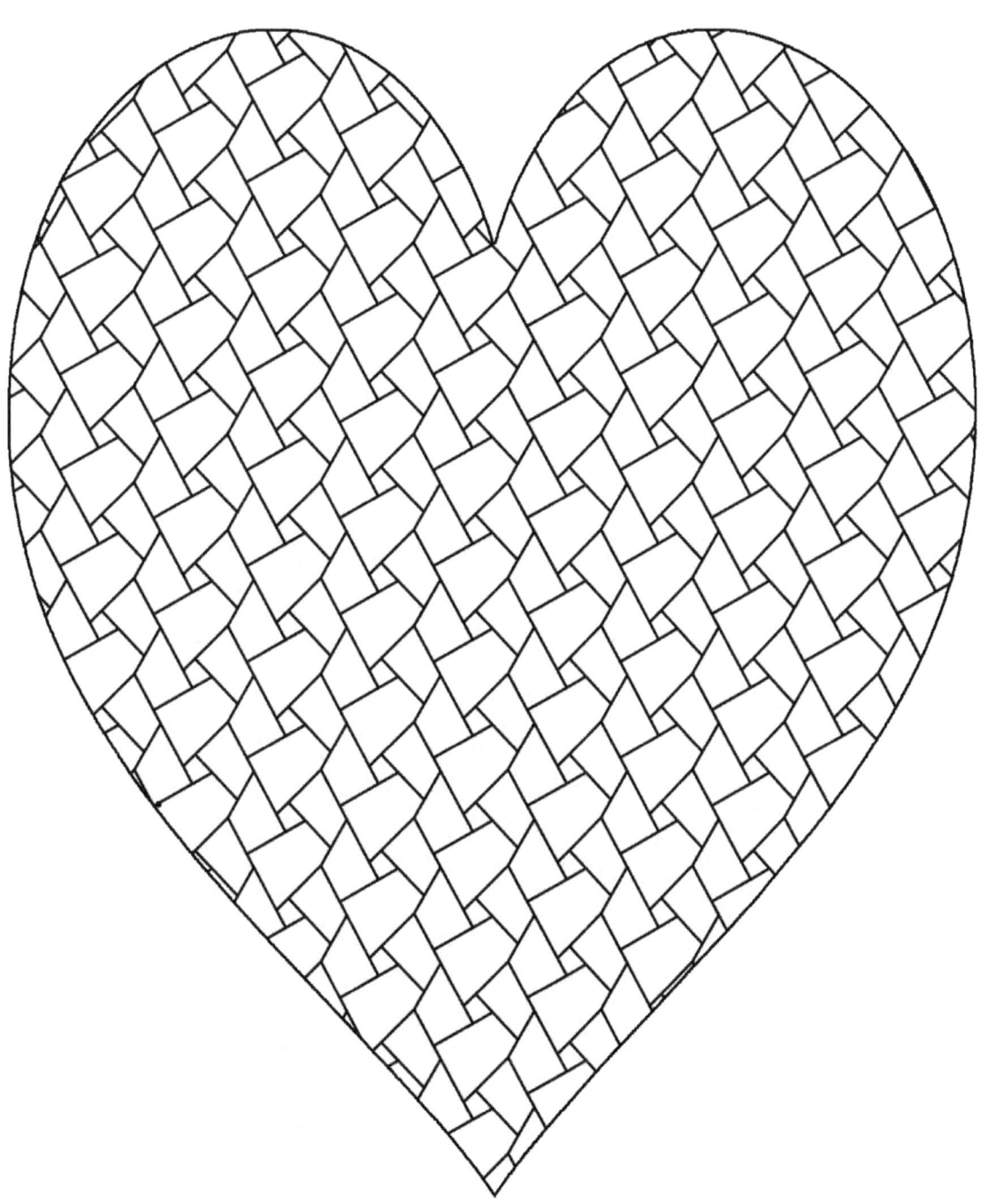

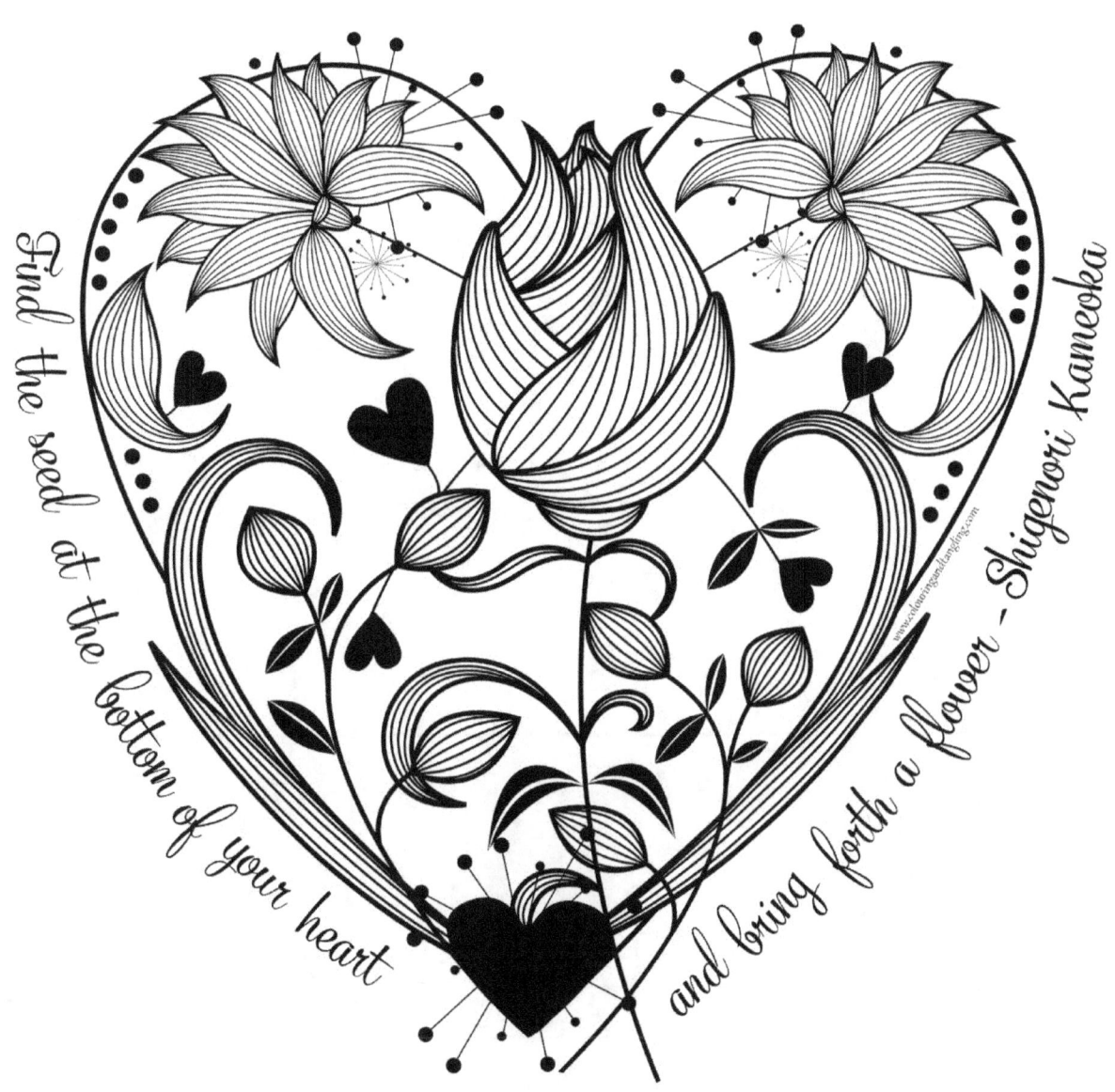

Find the seed at the bottom of your heart and bring forth a flower - Shigenori Kameoka

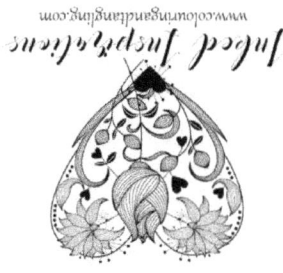

Inked Inspirations
www.colouringandtangling.com

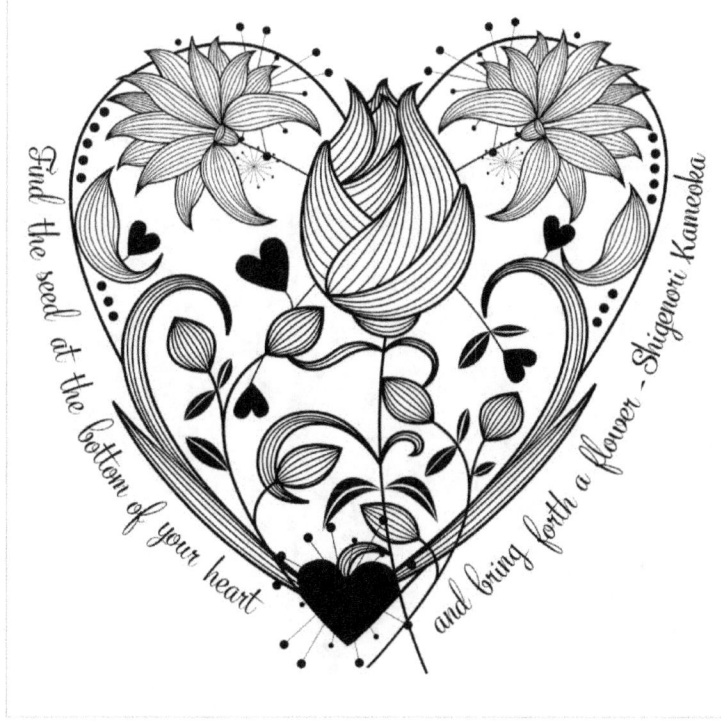

Find the seed at the bottom of your heart and bring forth a flower - Shigenori Kameoka

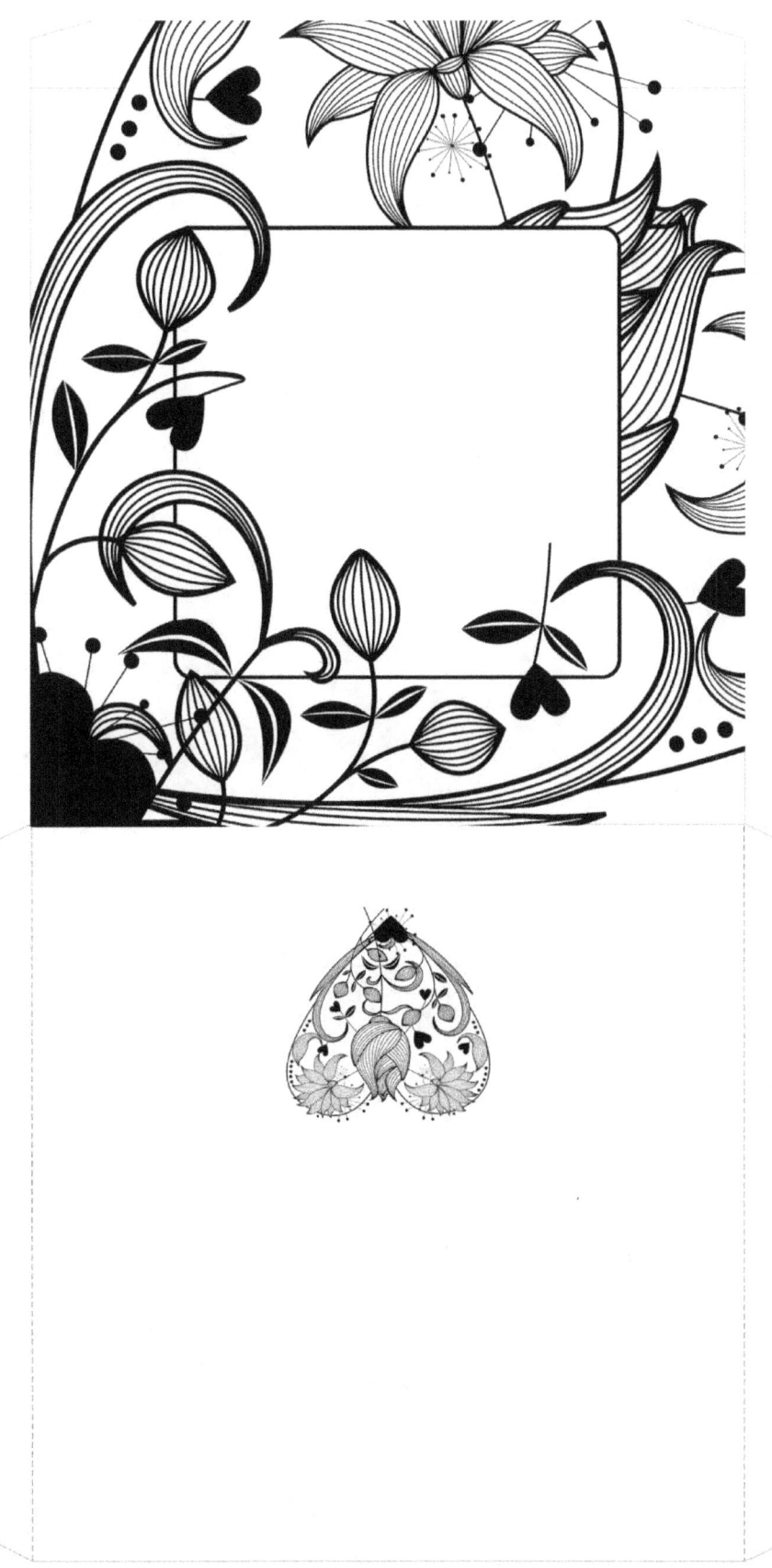

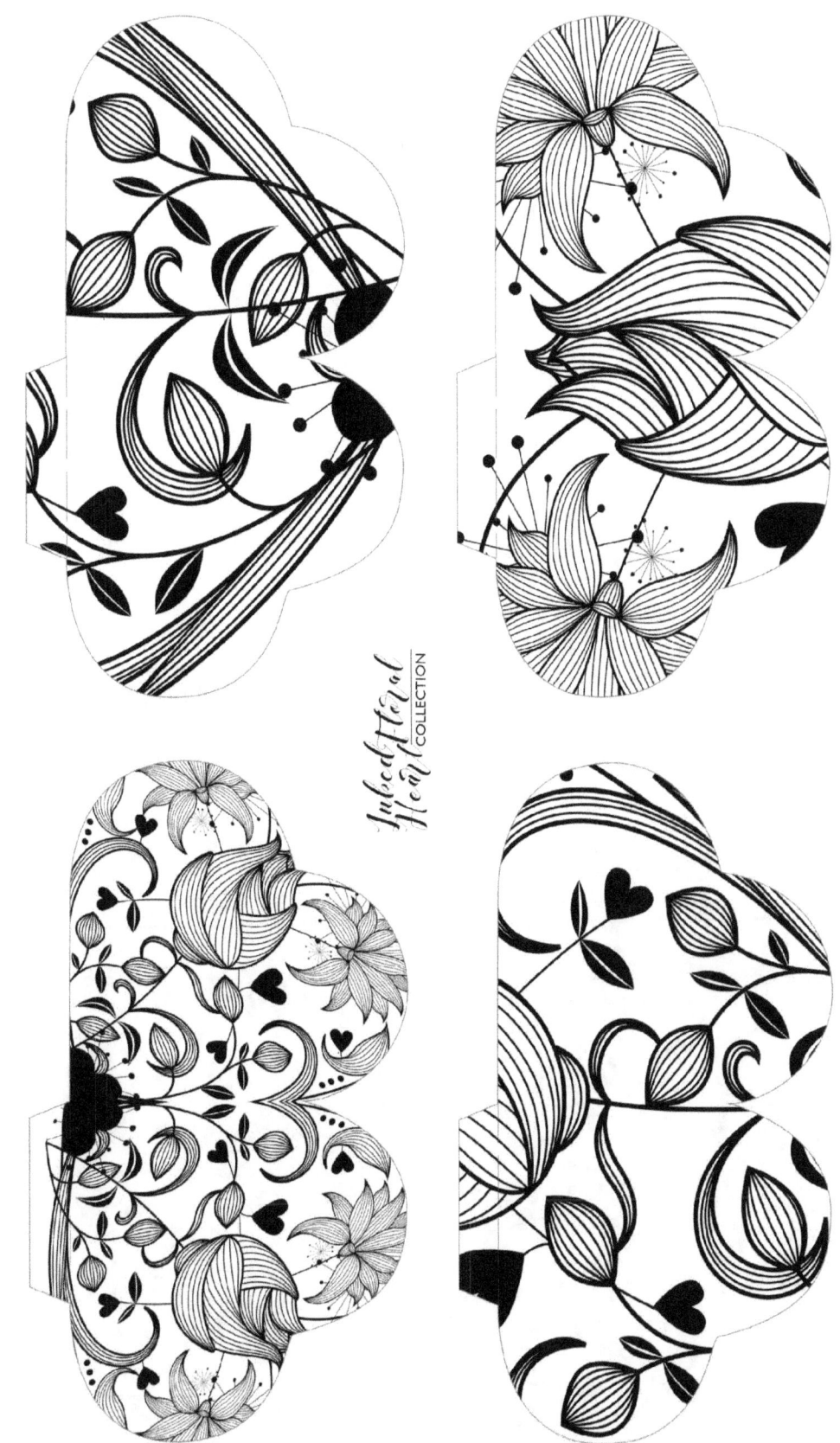

CORNER HEART BOOKMARKS

Inked Inspirations
www.colouringandtangling.com

Inked Heart COLLECTION

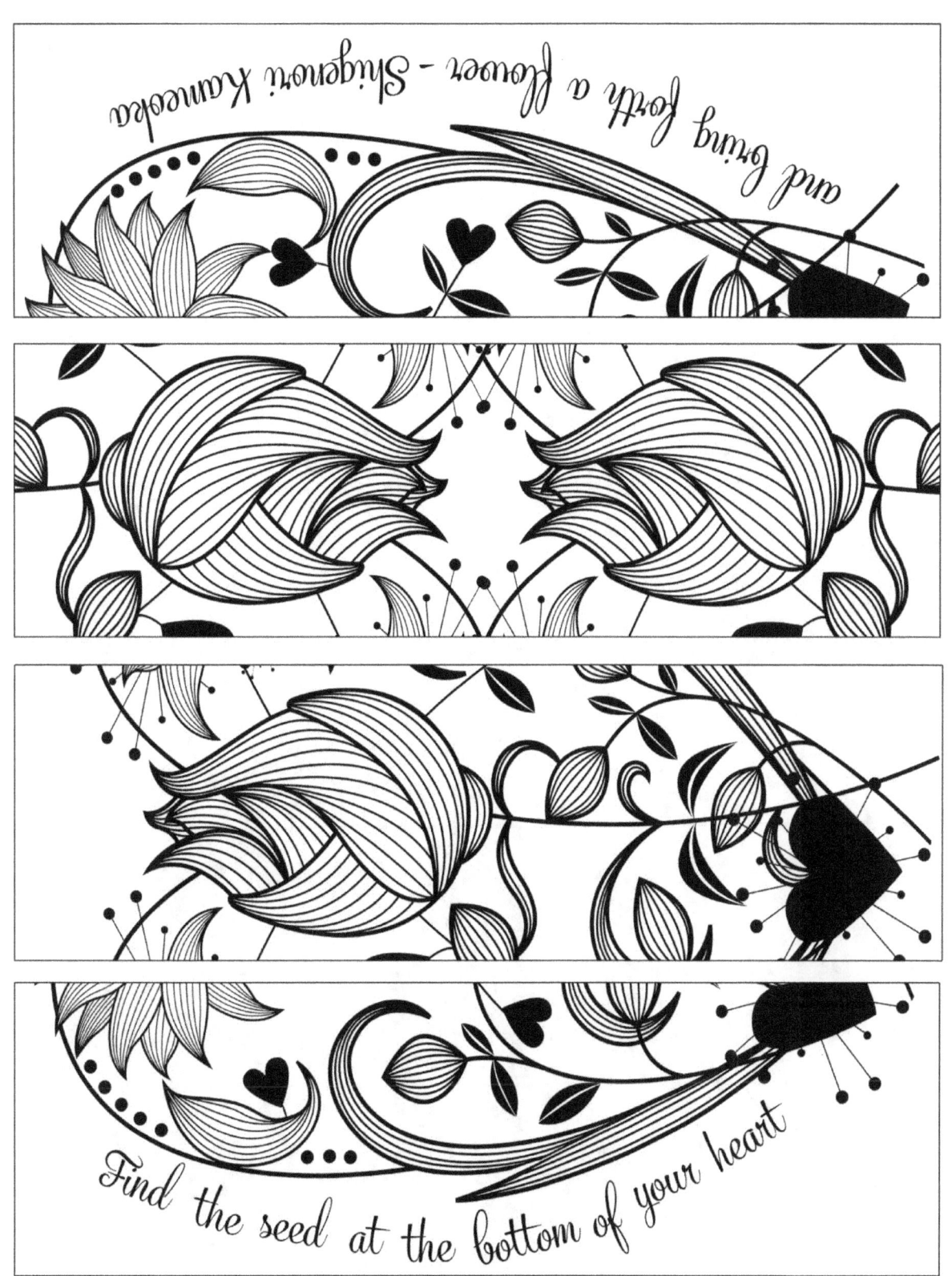

and bring forth a flower - Shigenori Kameoka

Find the seed at the bottom of your heart

"Inked Floral Heart" by Lesley Smitheringale at www.colouringandtangling.com

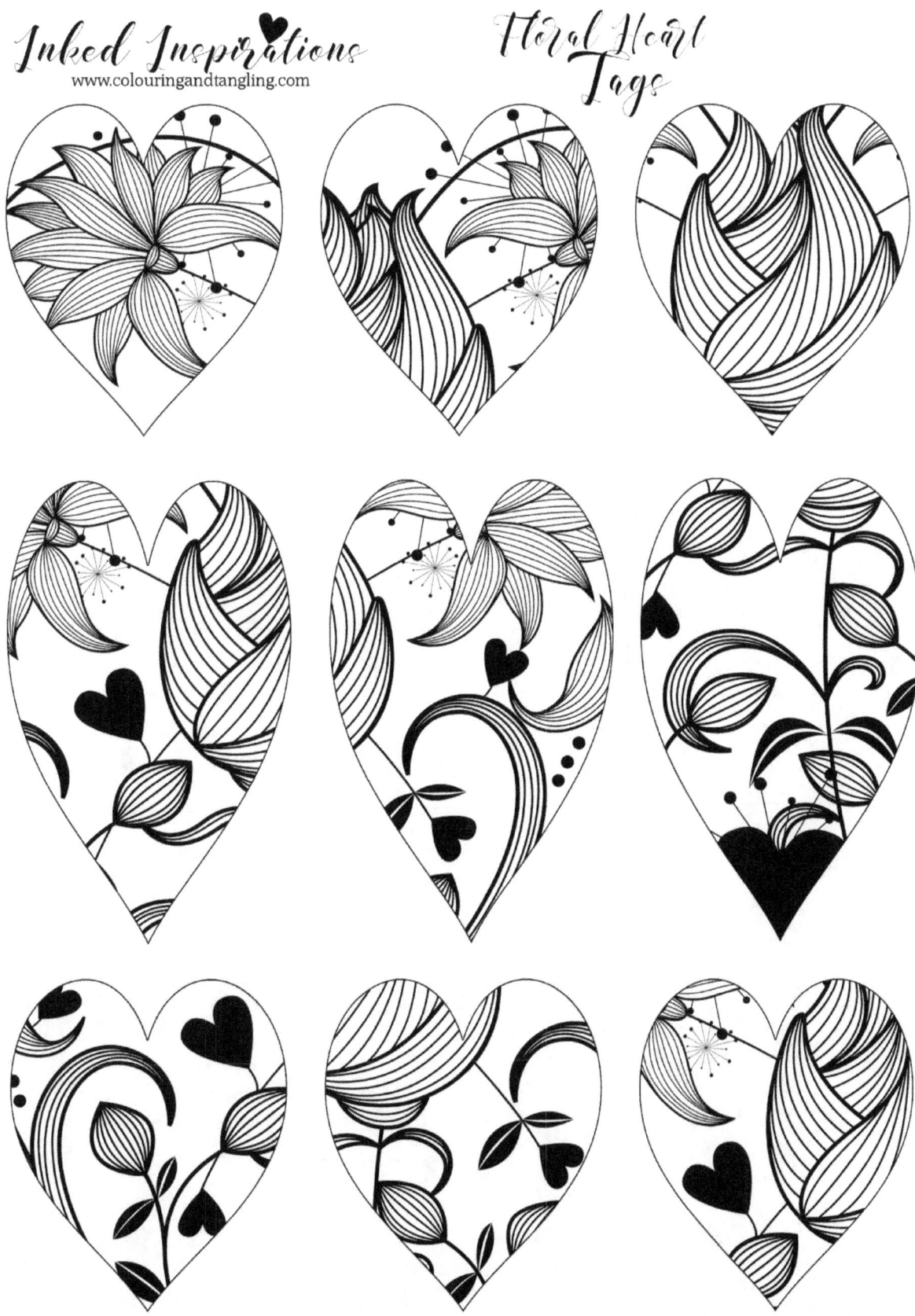

Inked Inspirations
www.colouringandtangling.com

Floral Heart Tags

Inked Inspirations
www.colouringandtangling.com

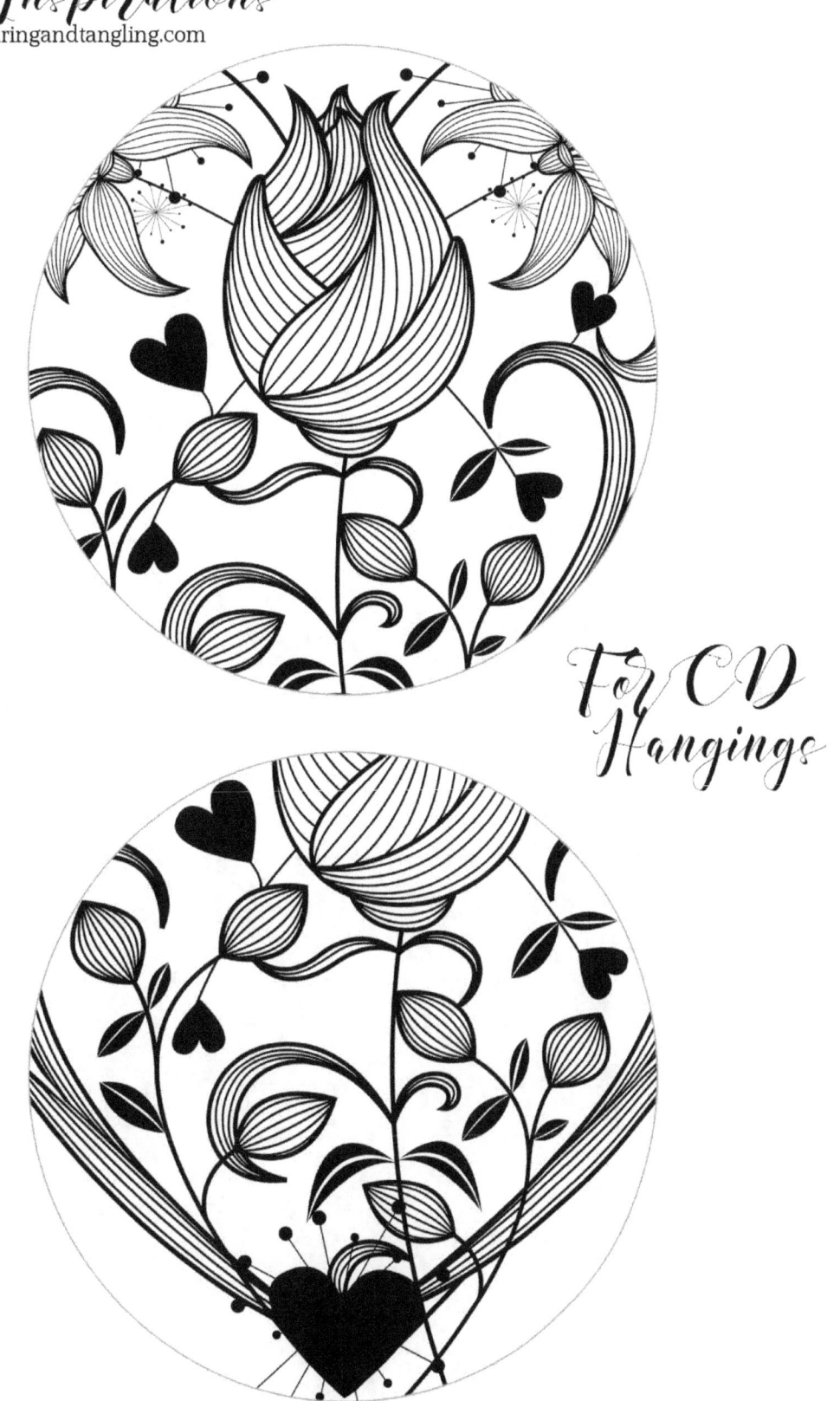

For CD
Hangings

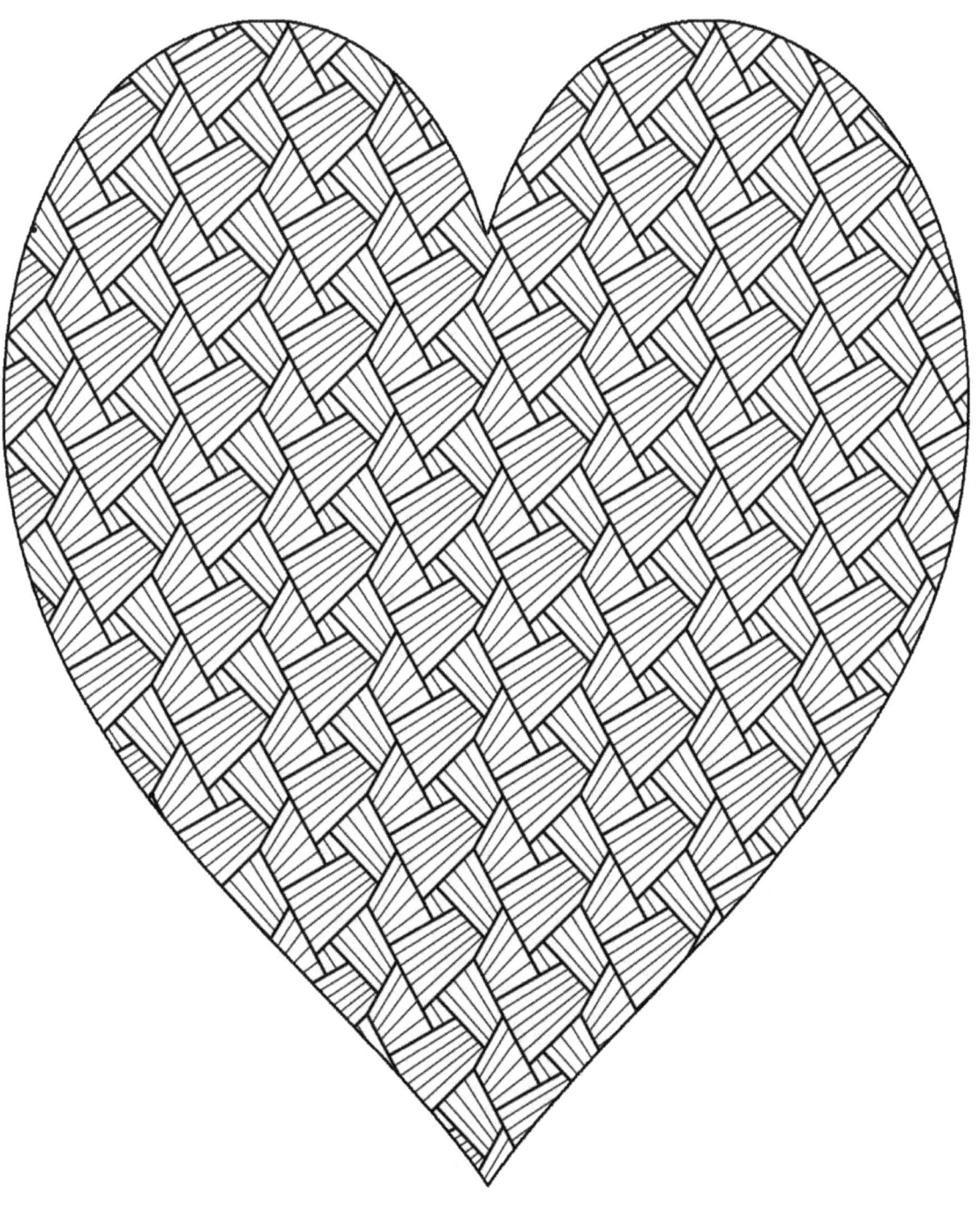

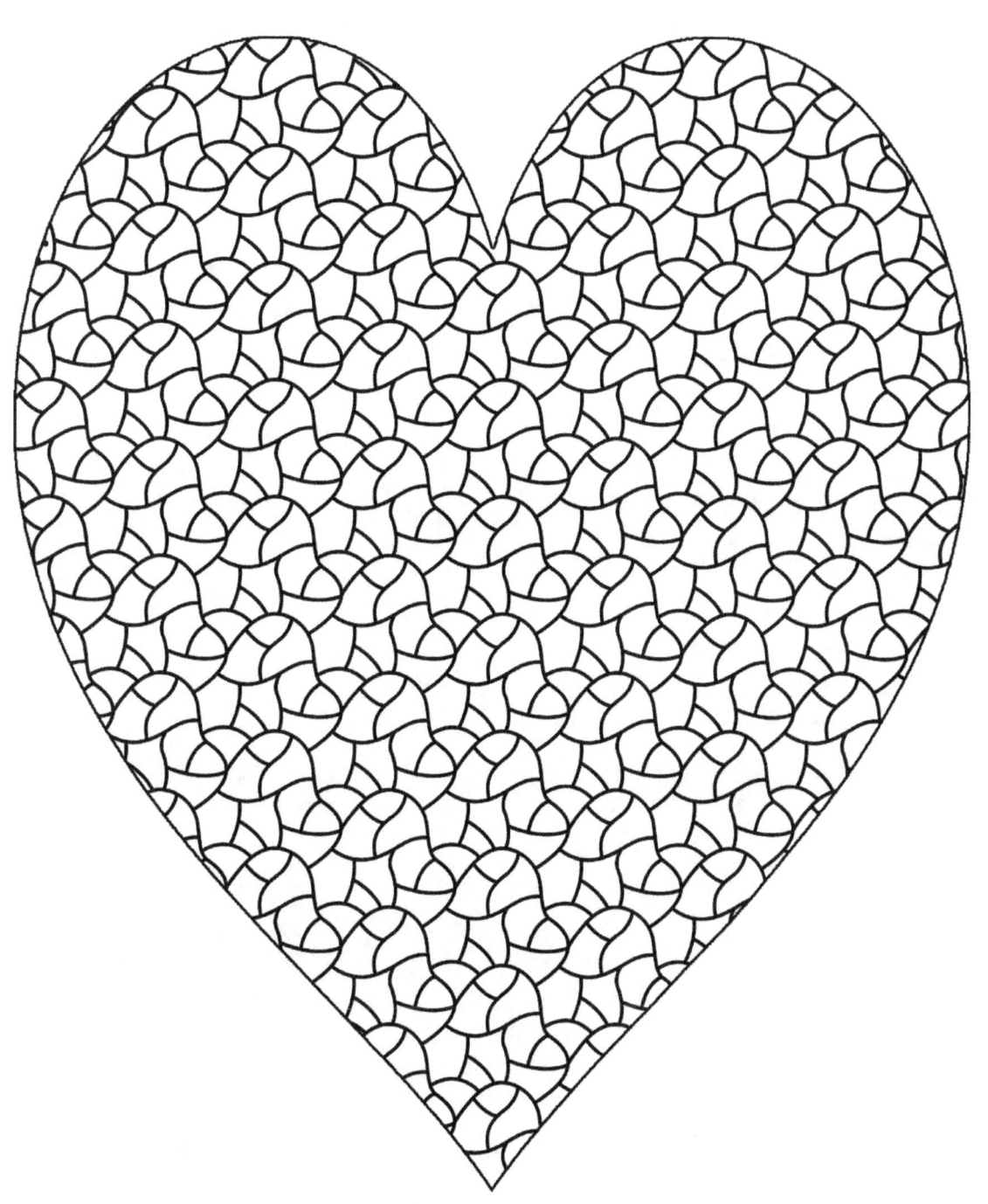

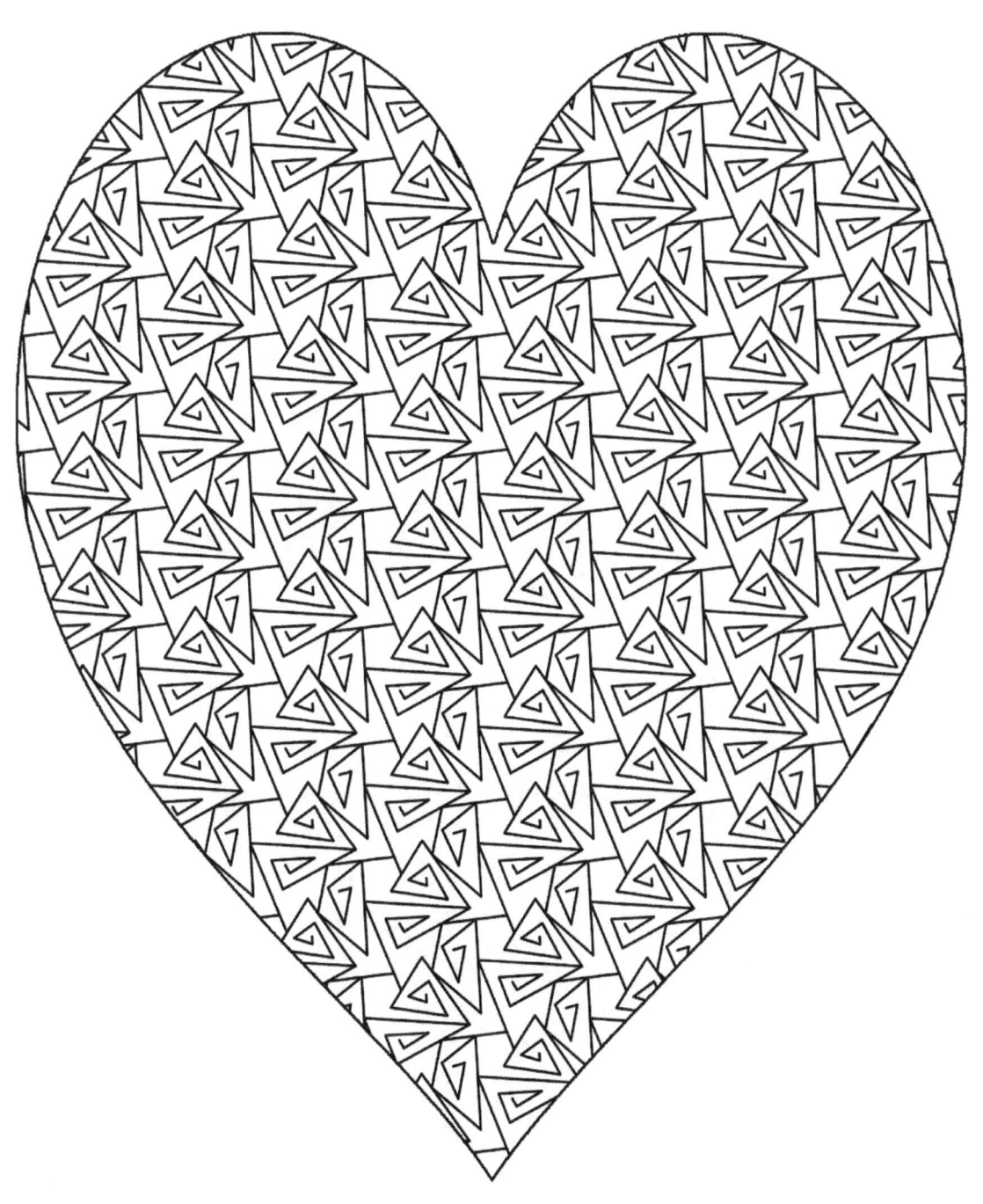

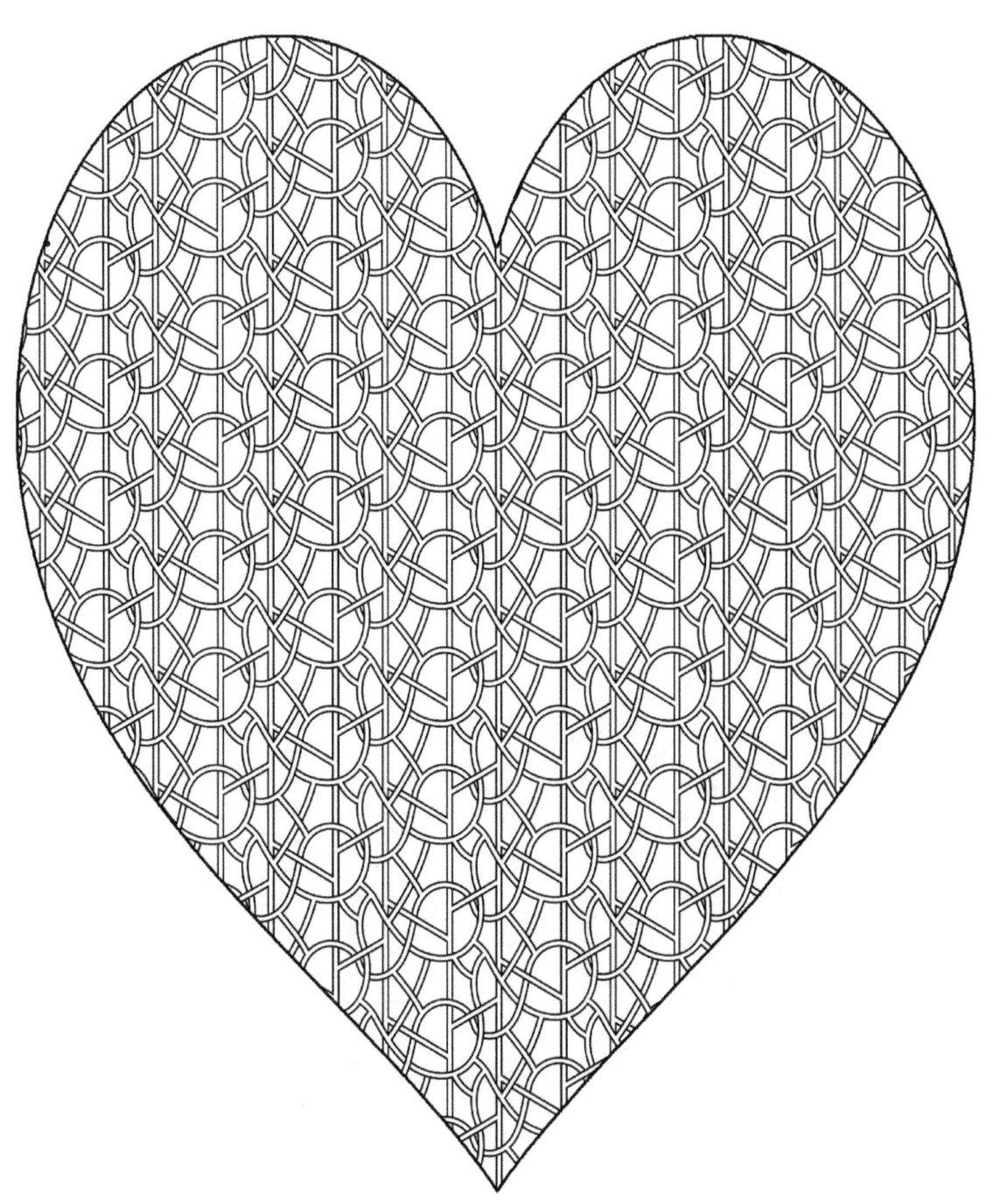

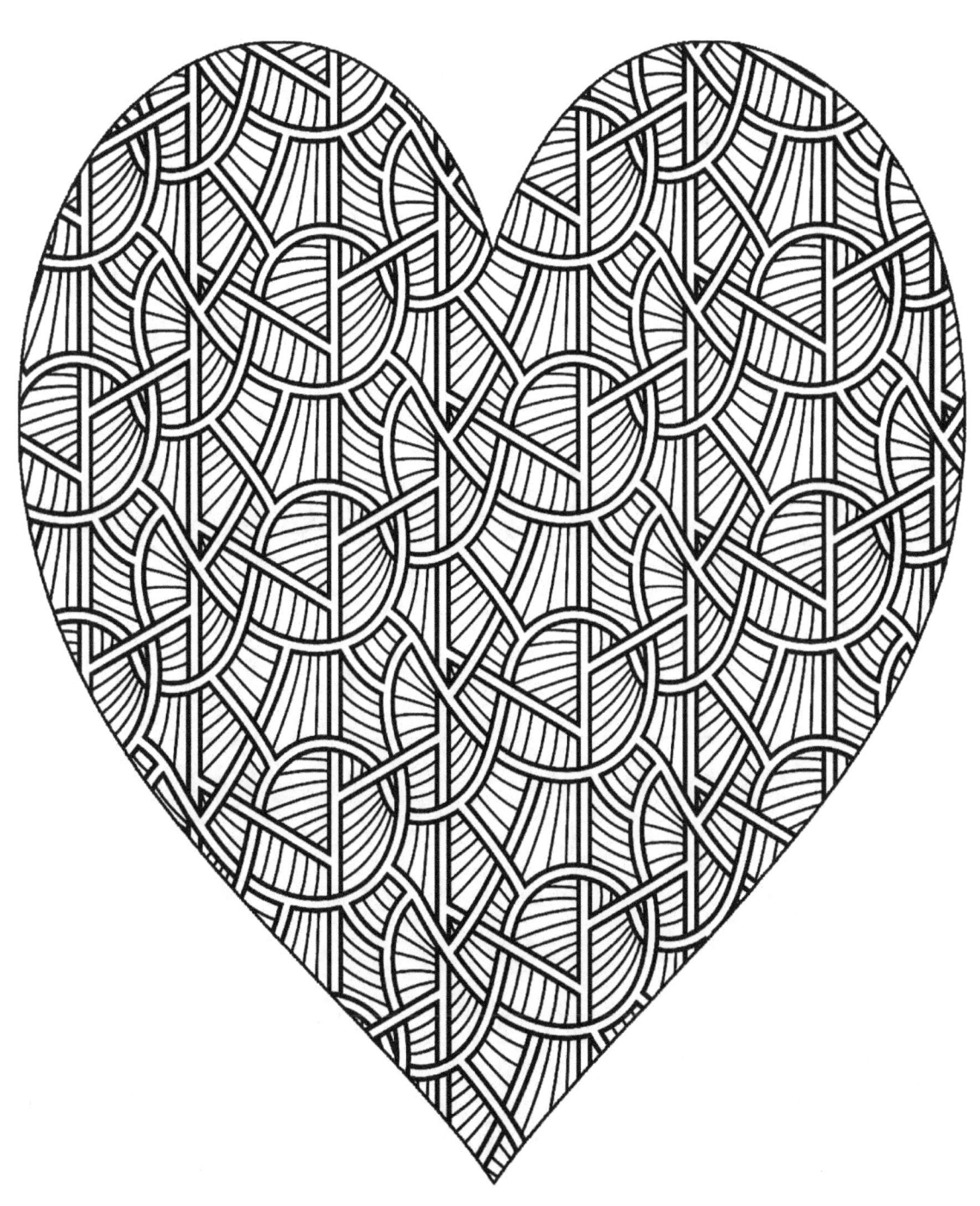

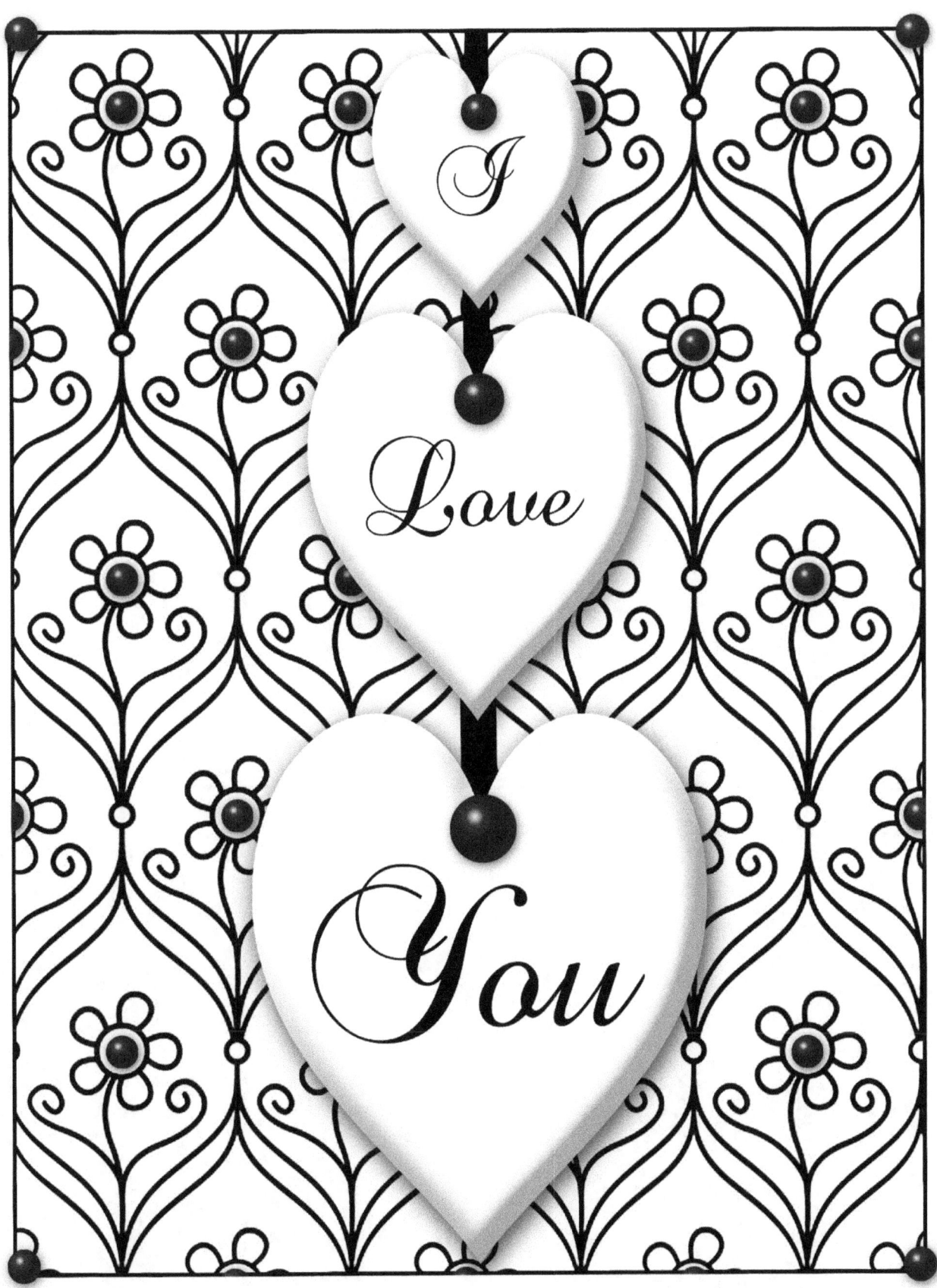

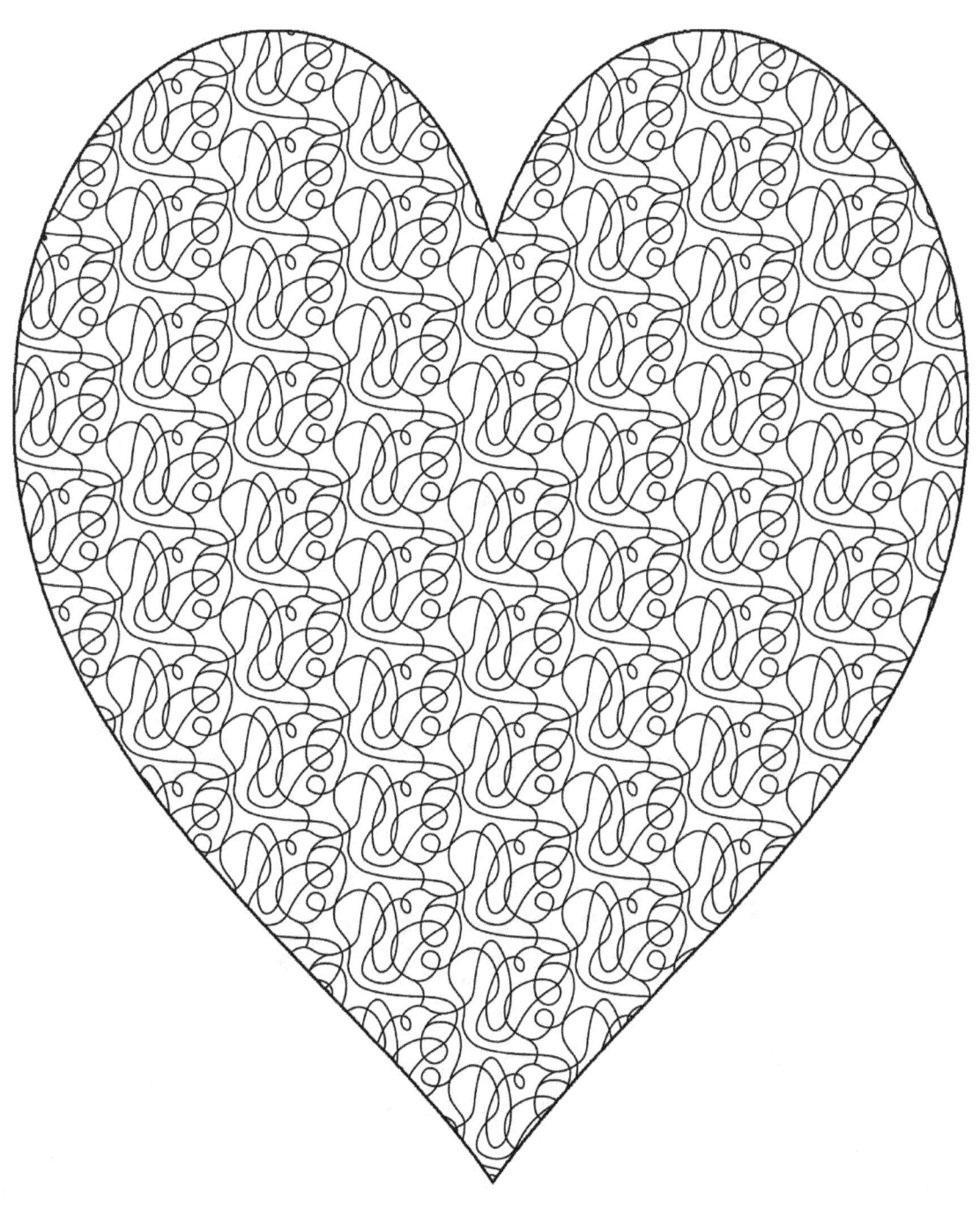

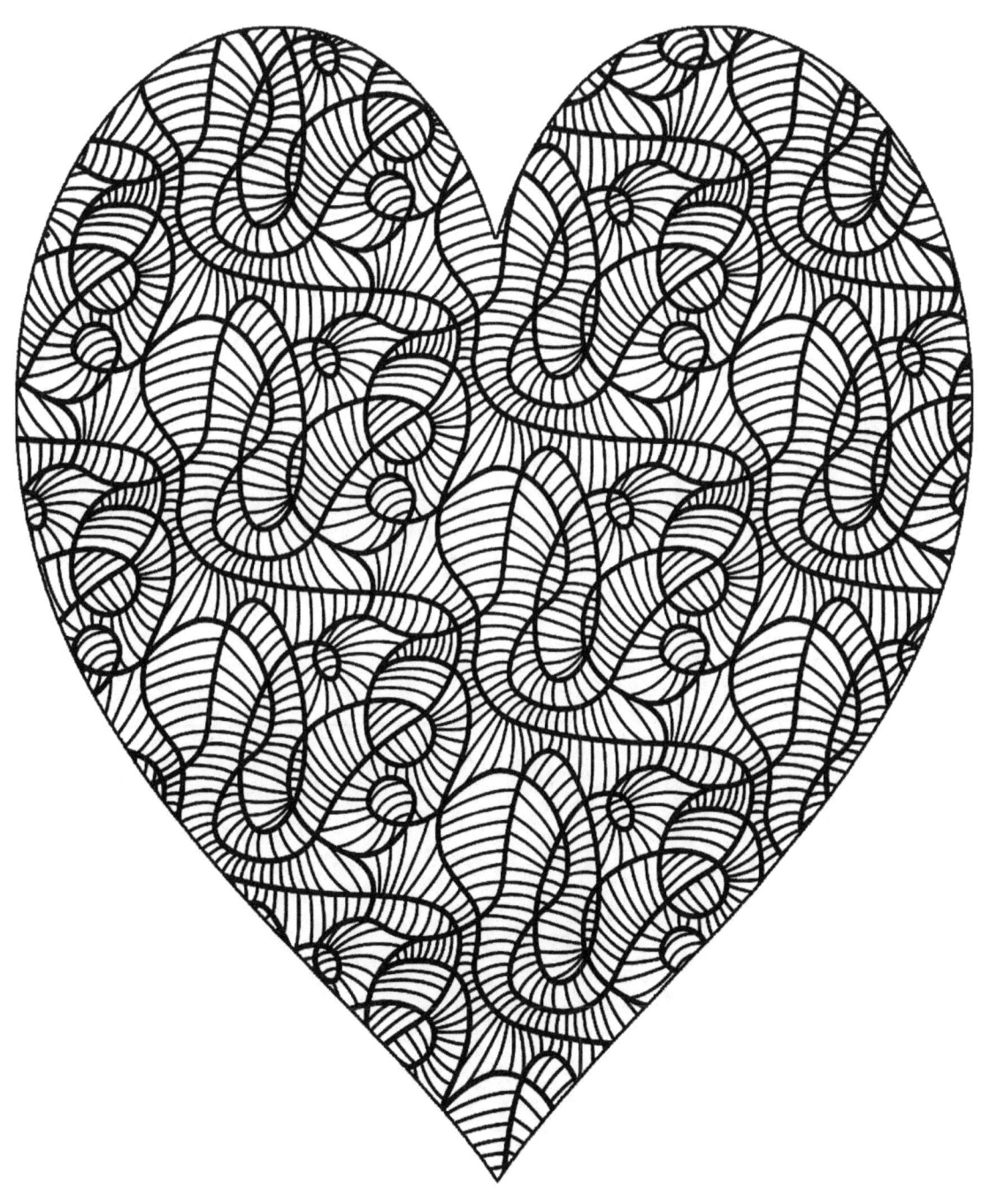

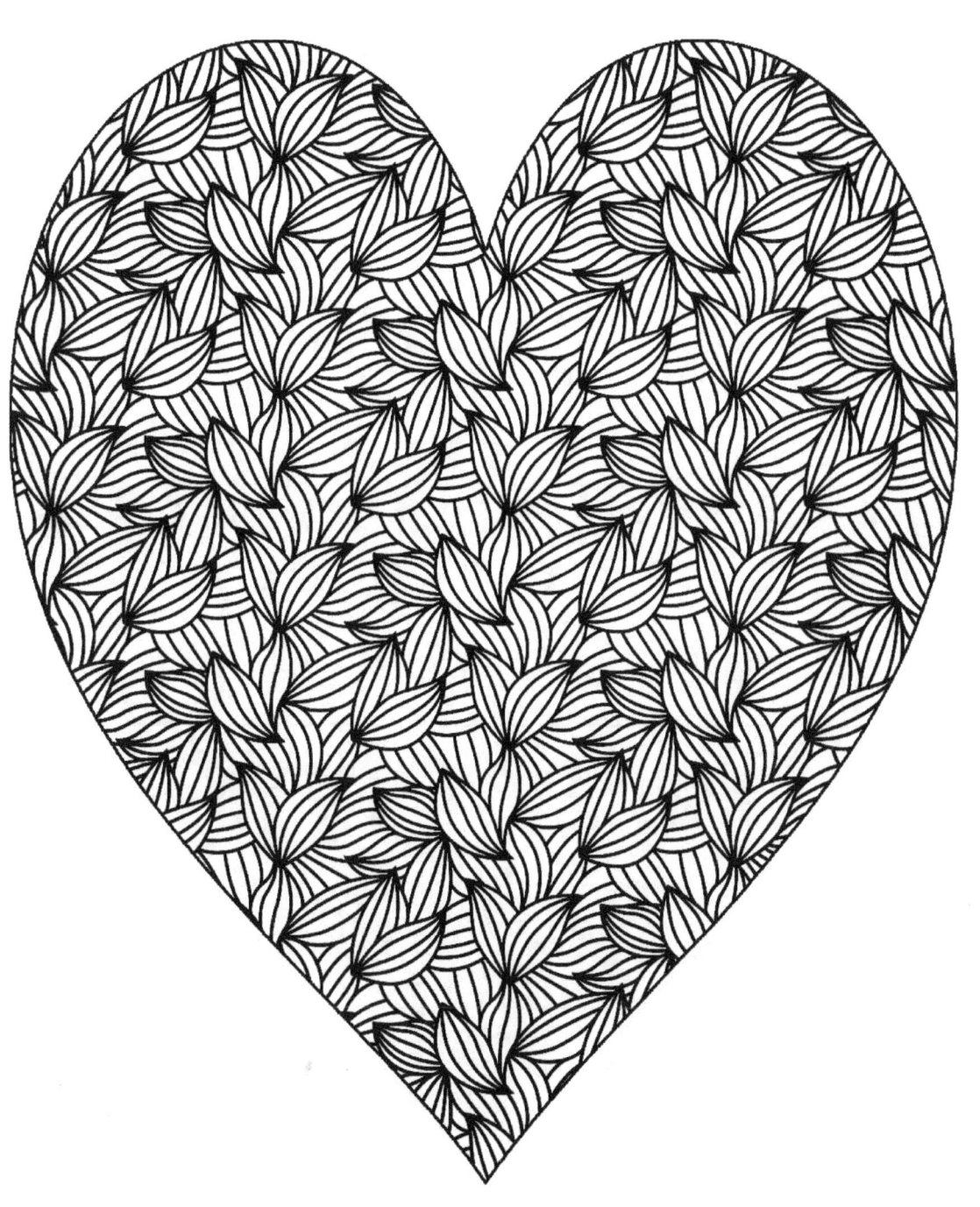

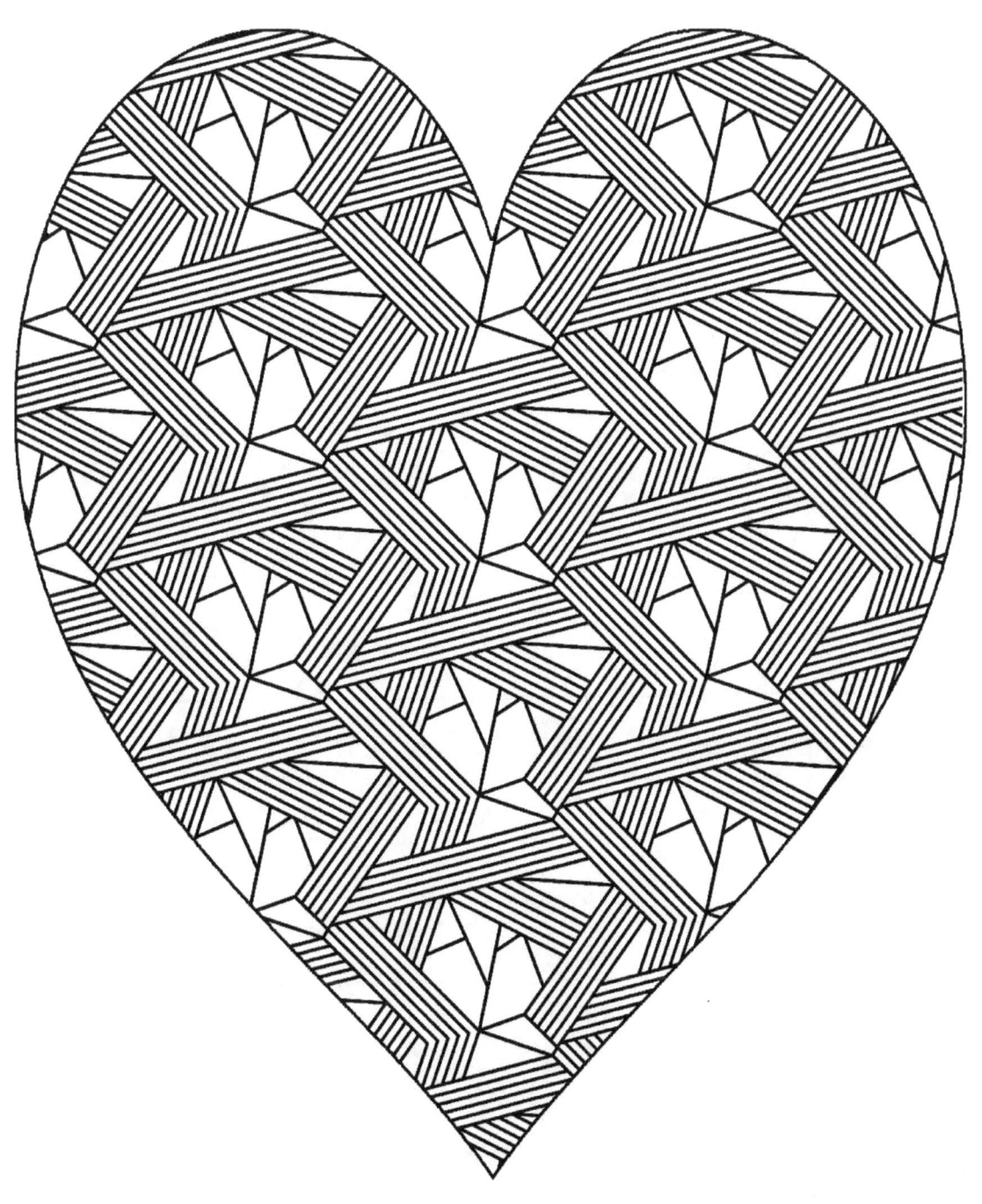

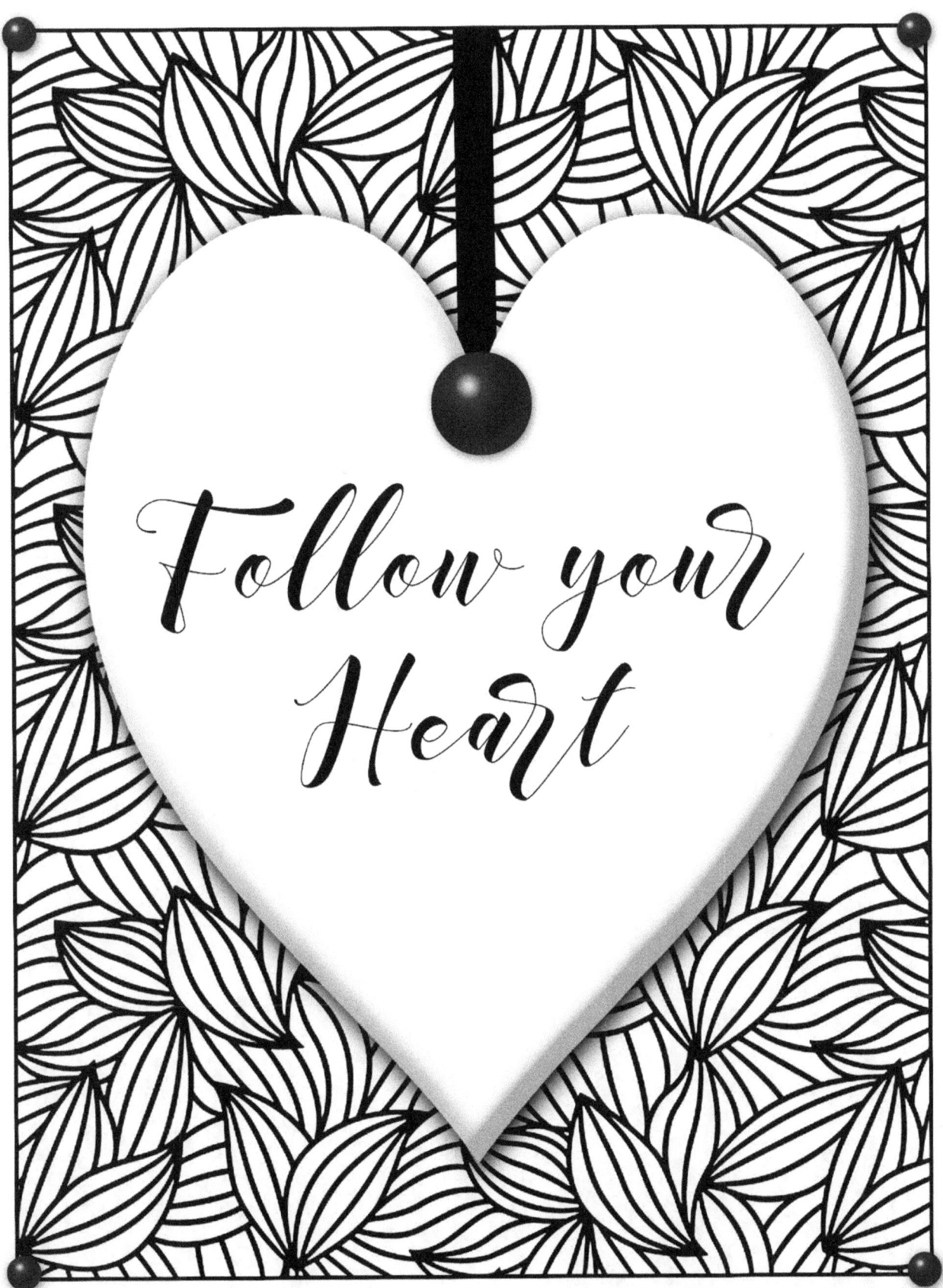

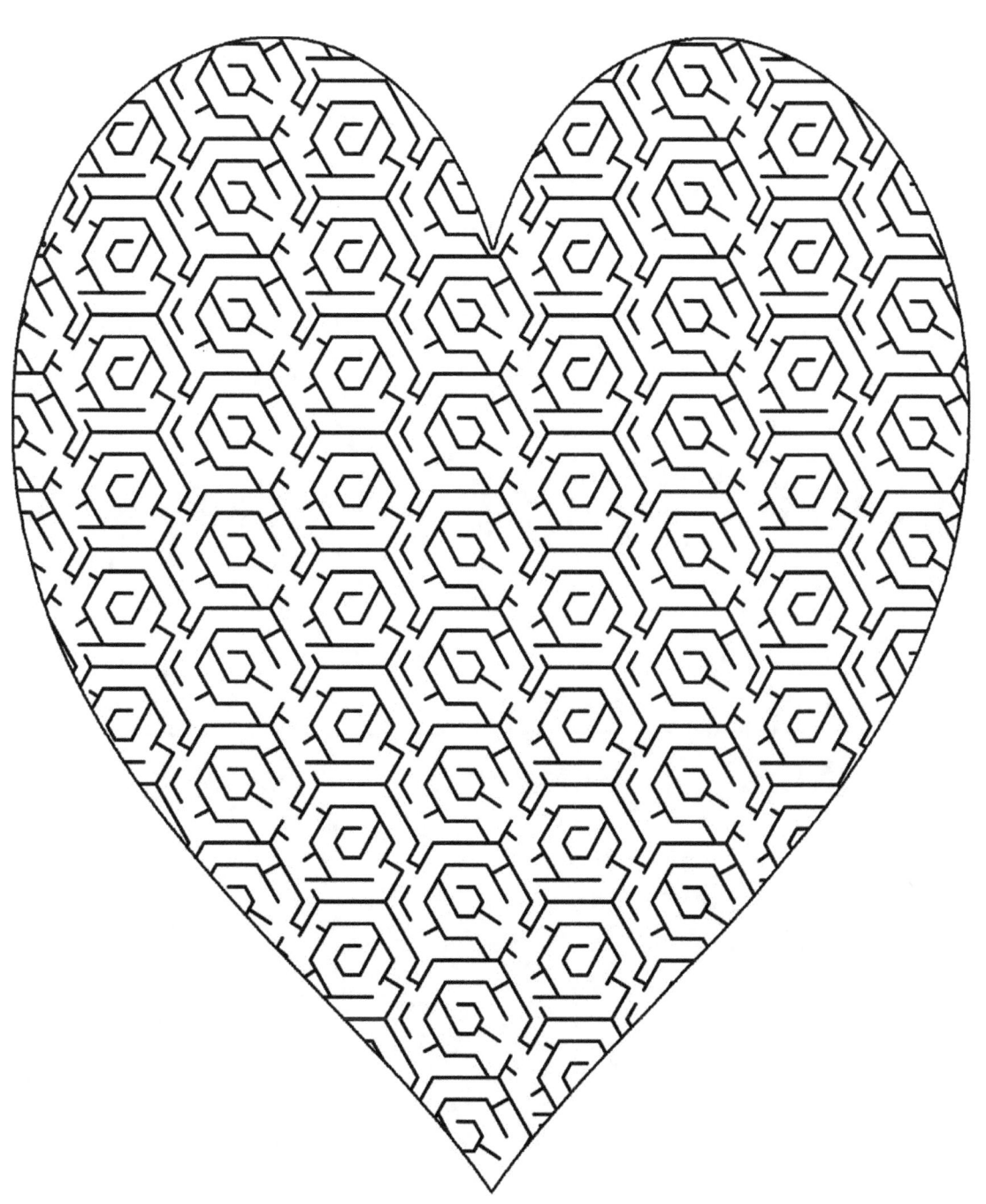

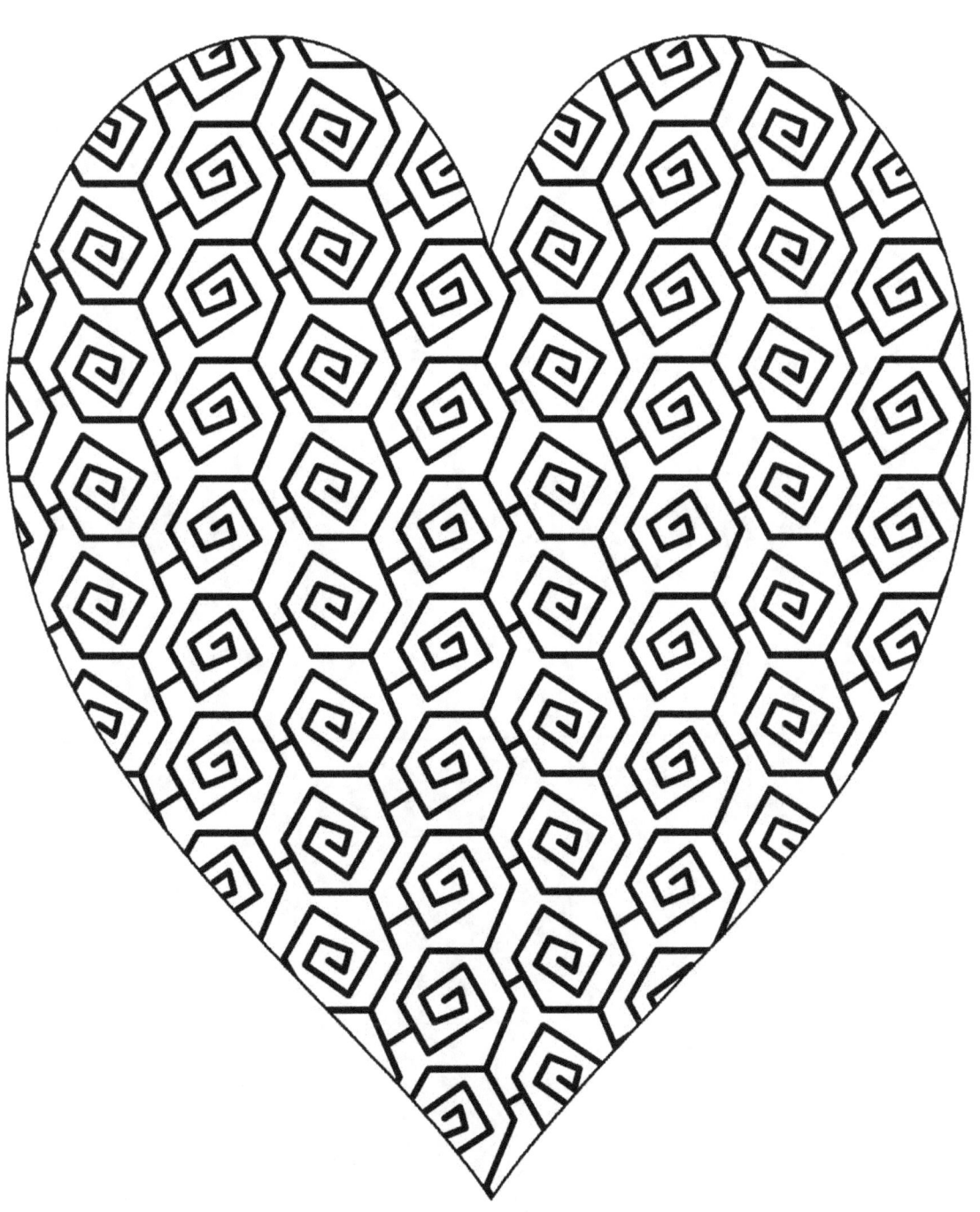

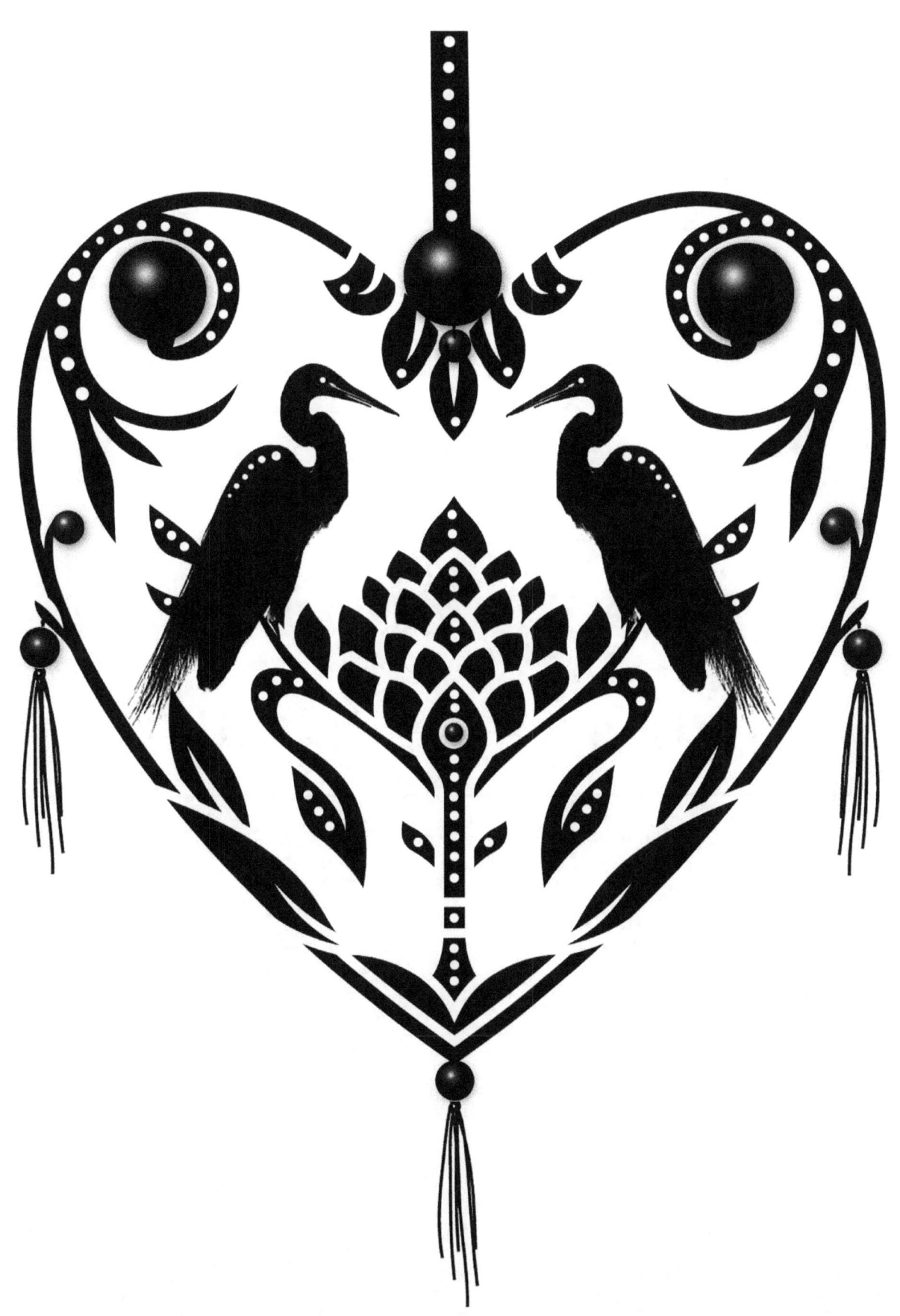

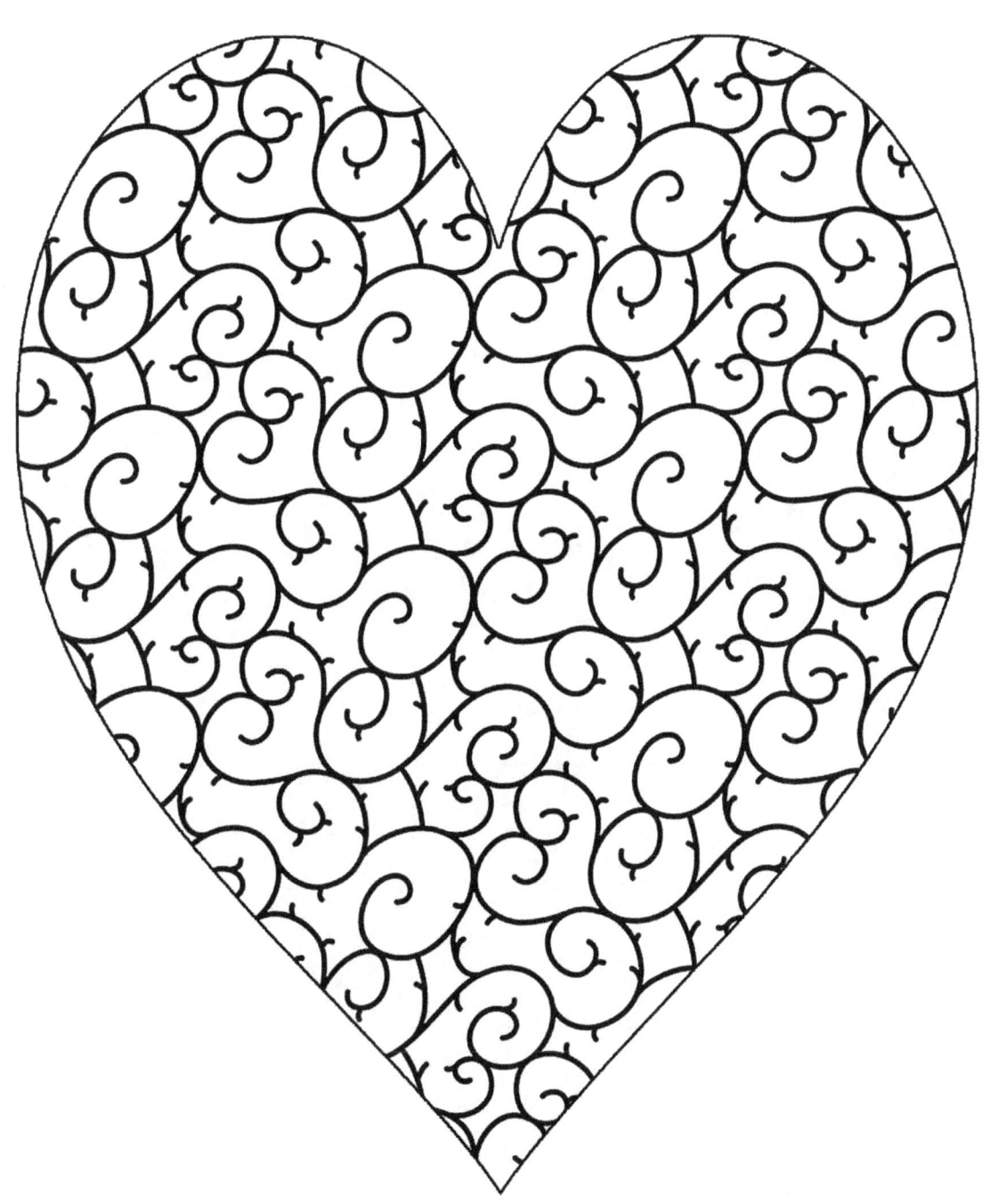

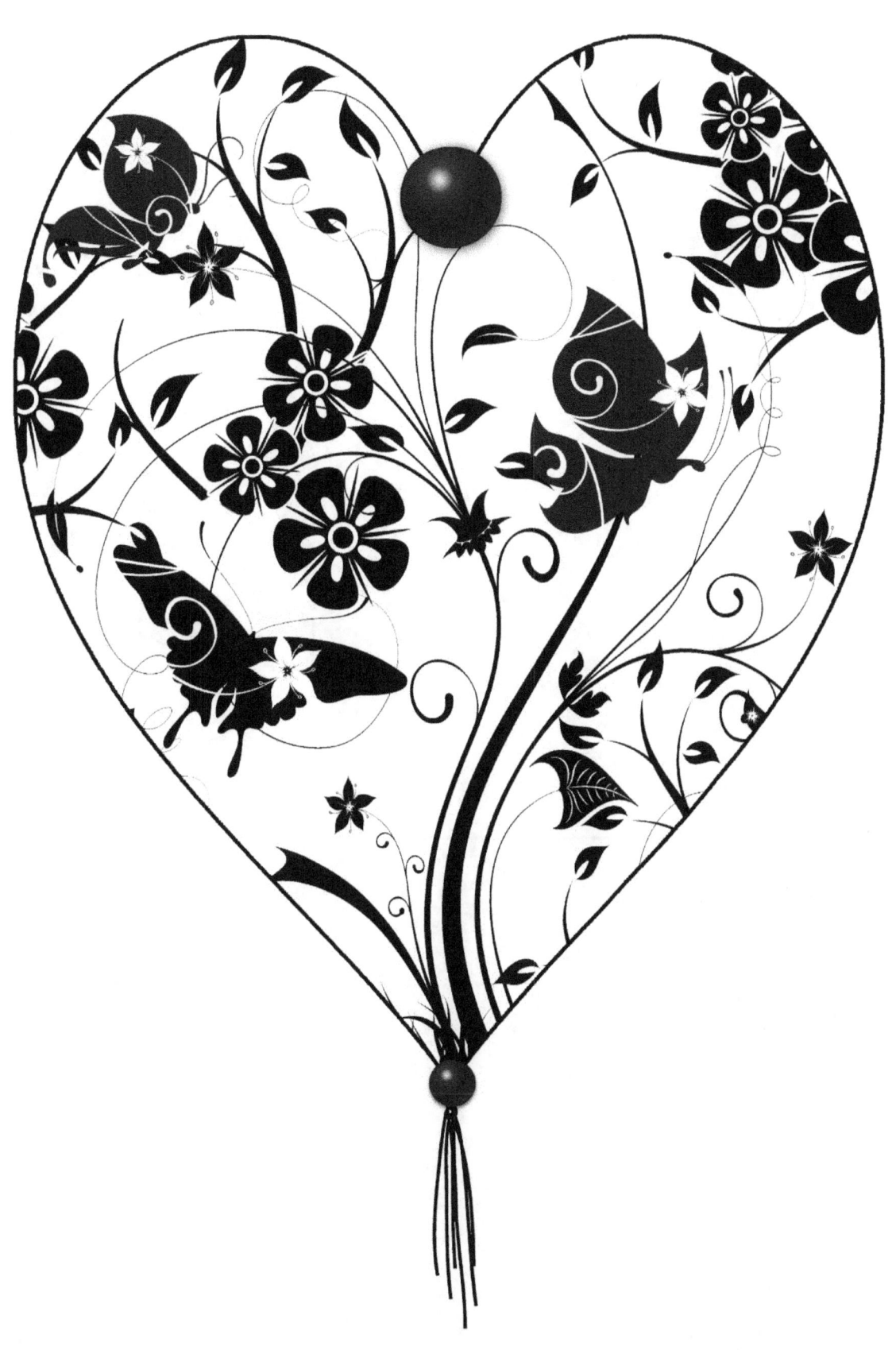

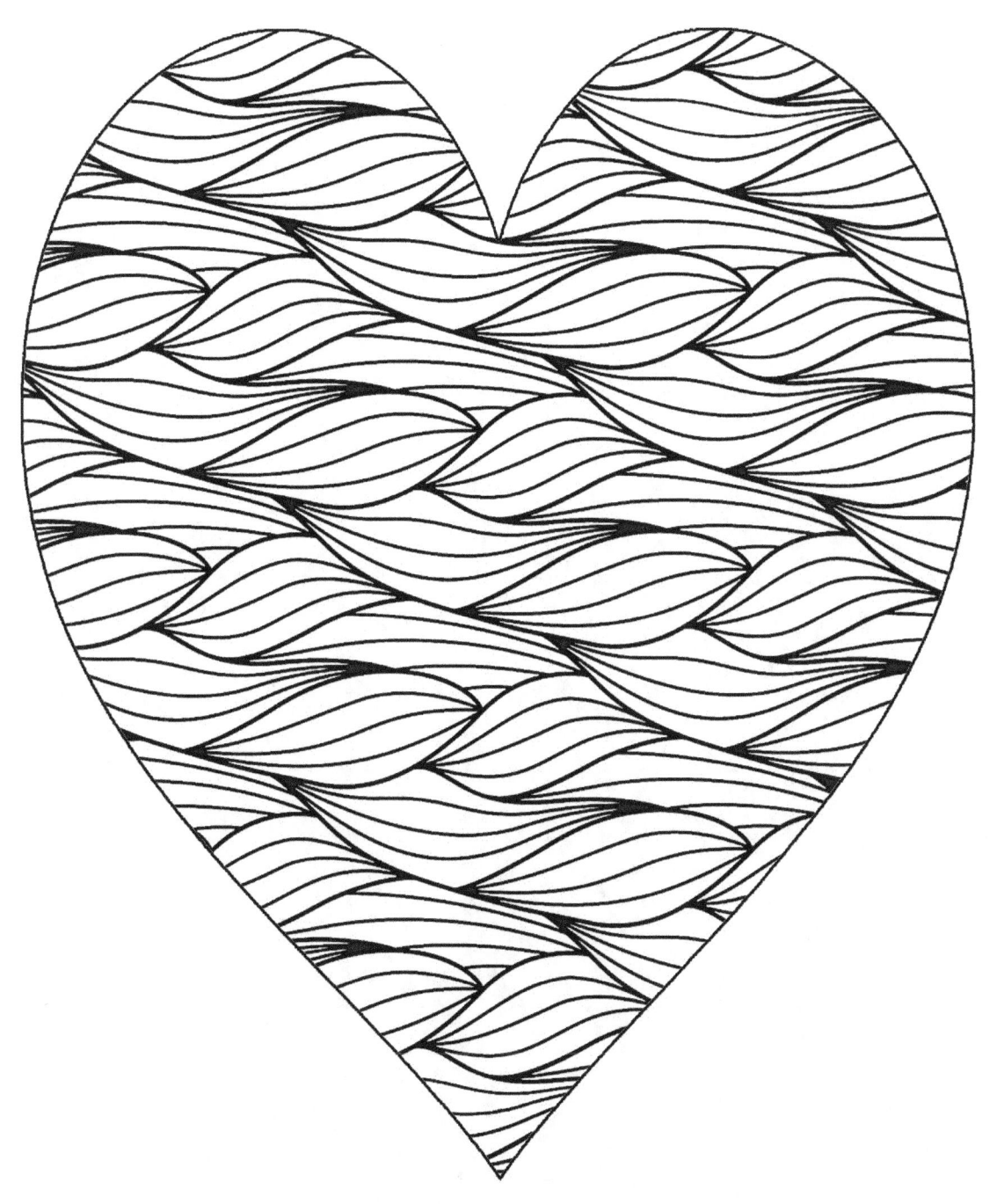

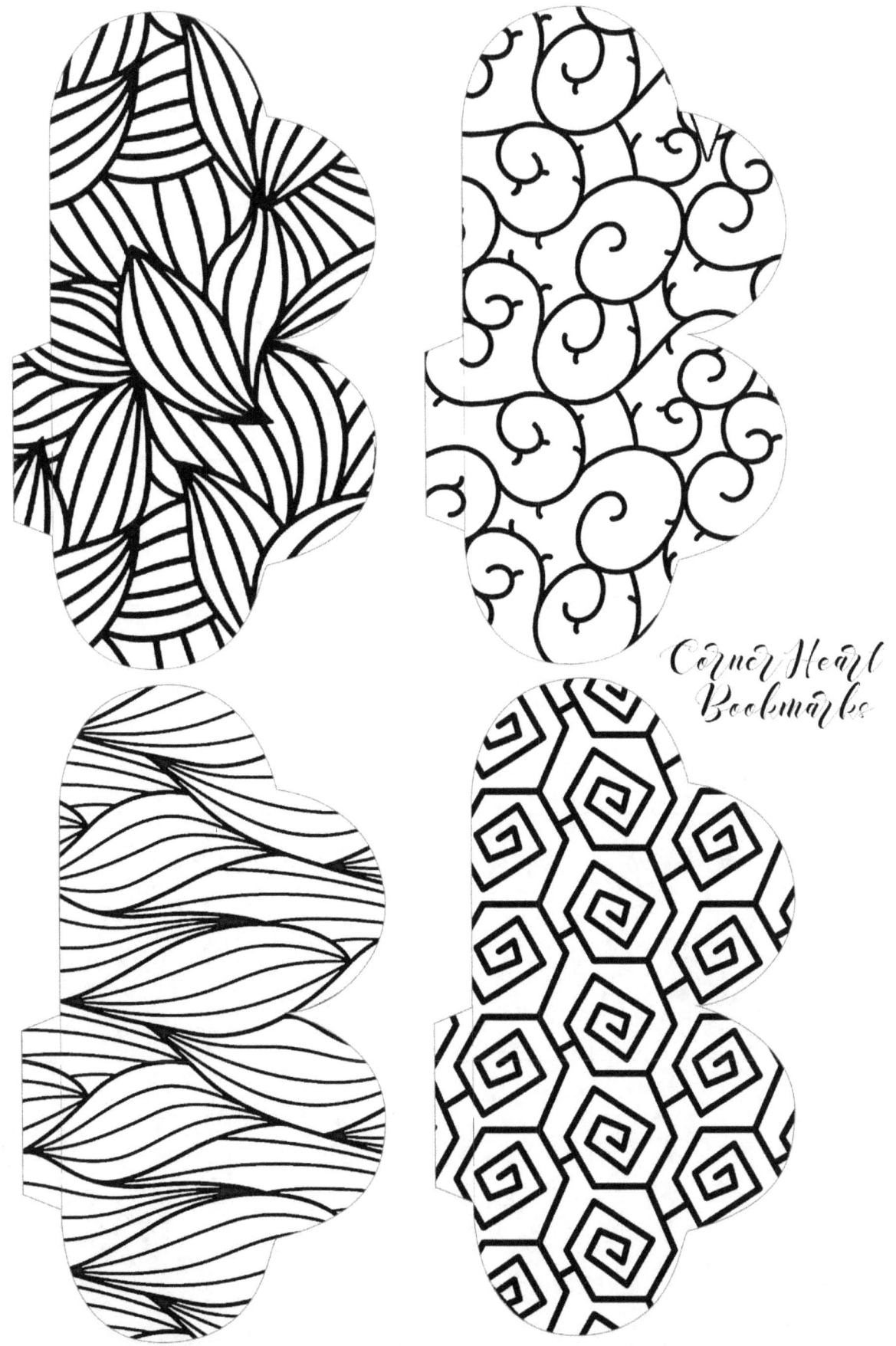

Corner Heart Bookmarks

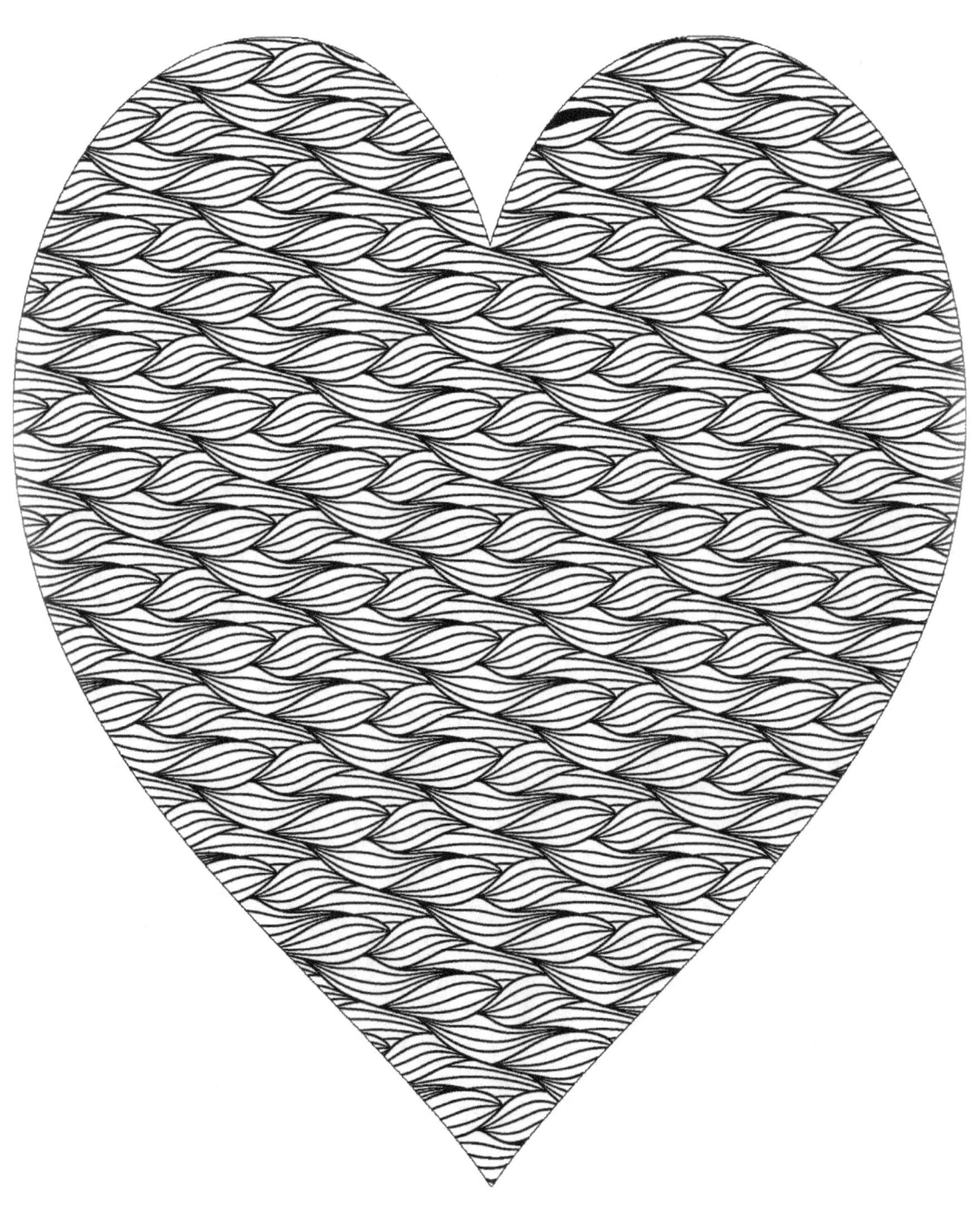

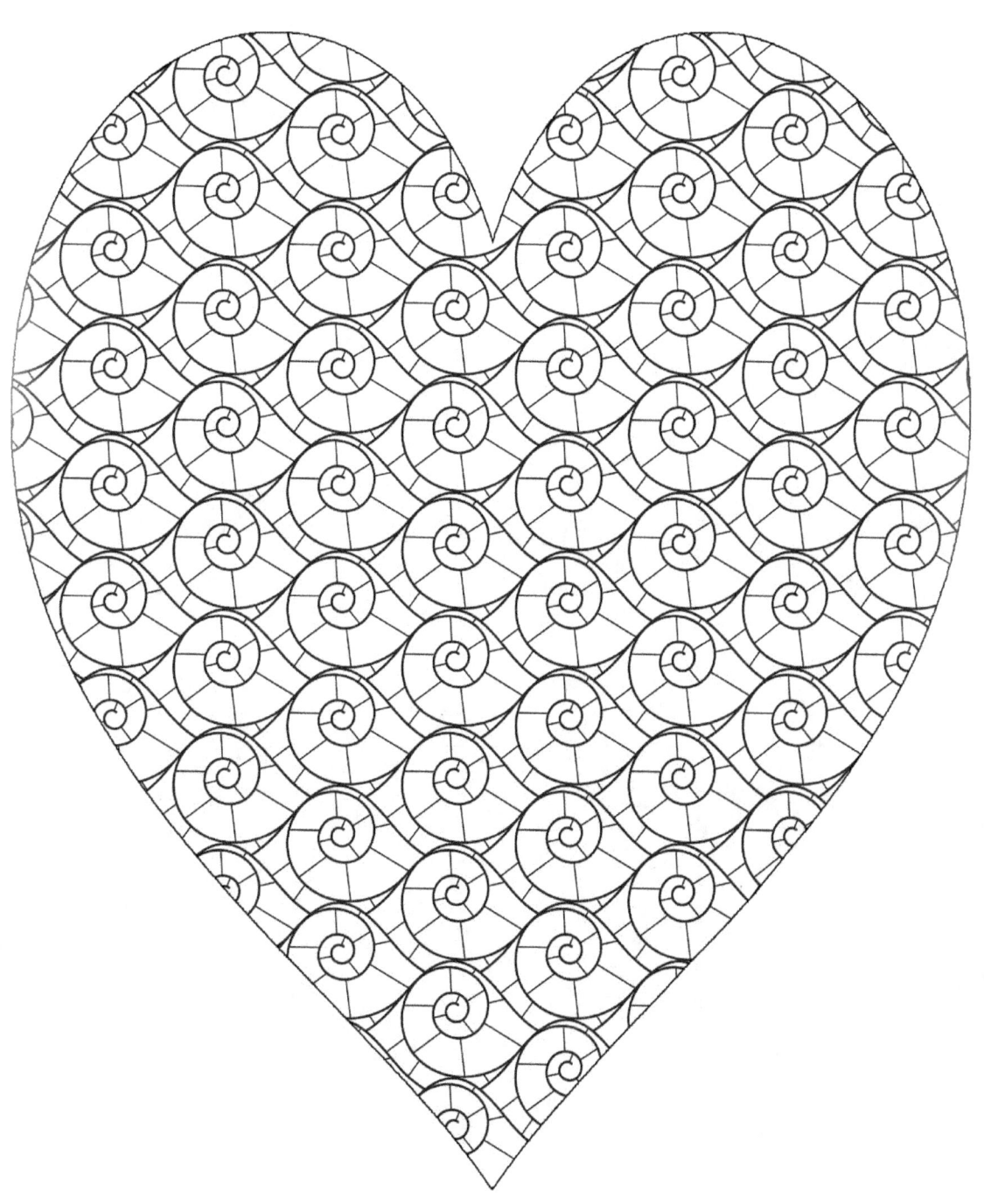

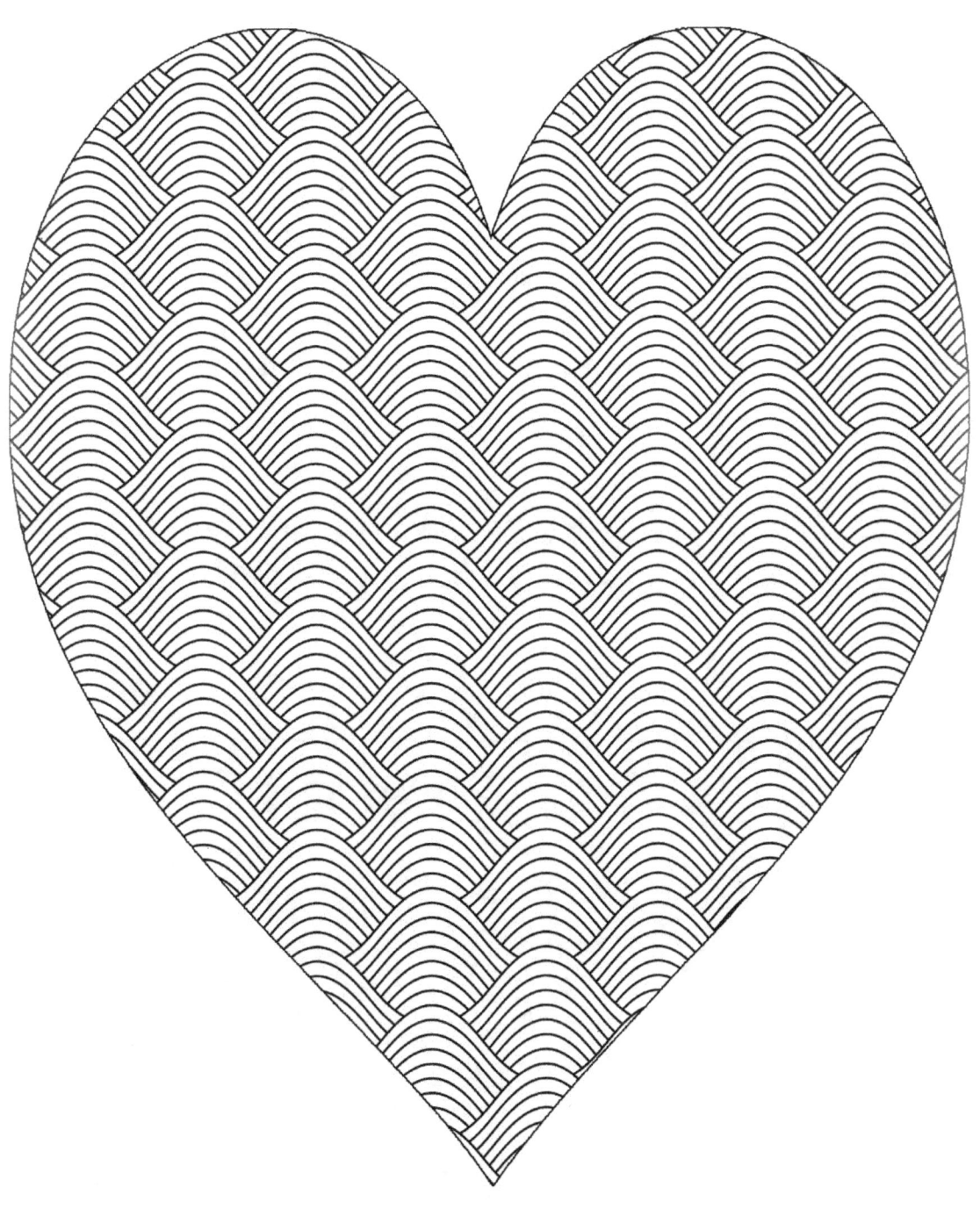

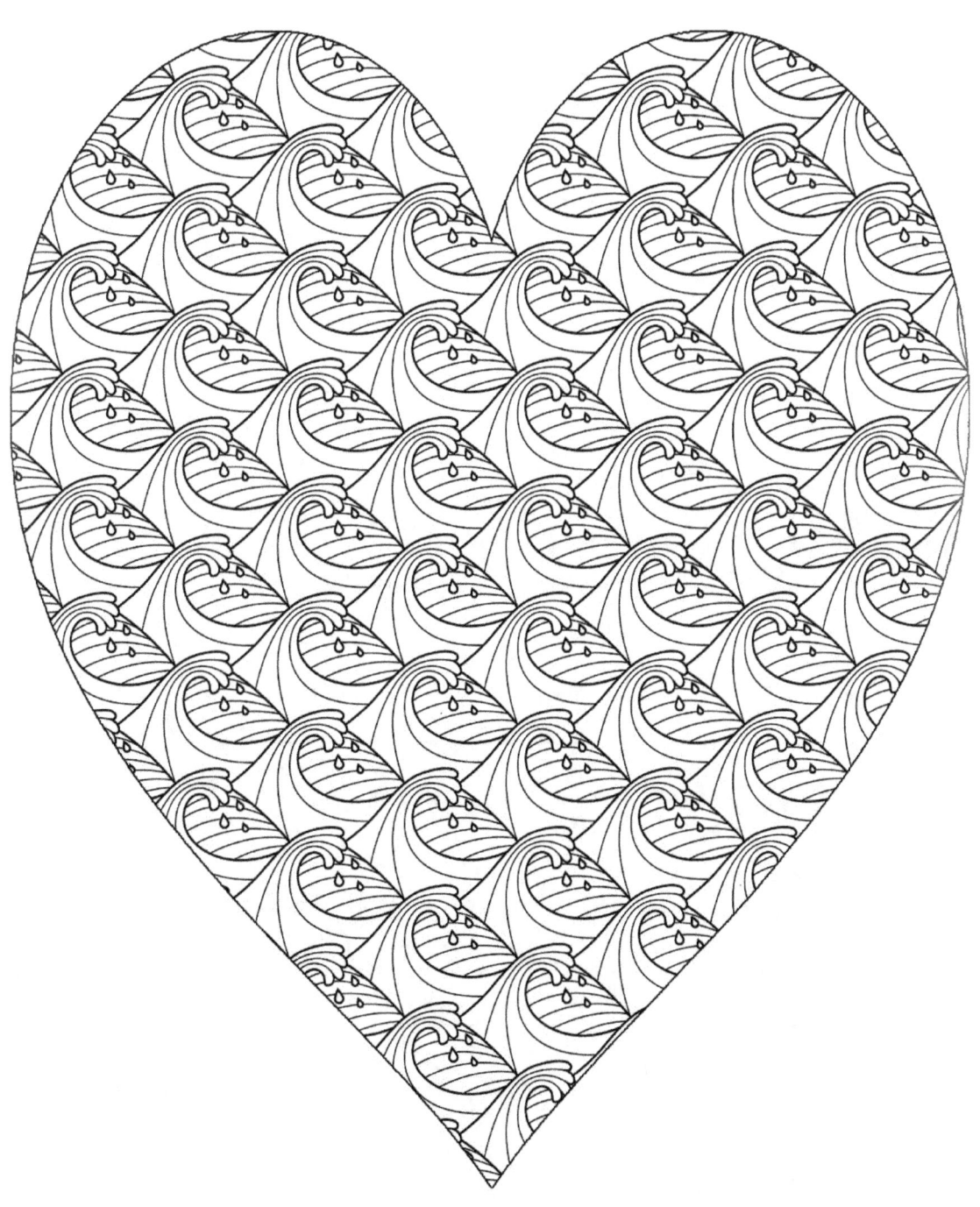

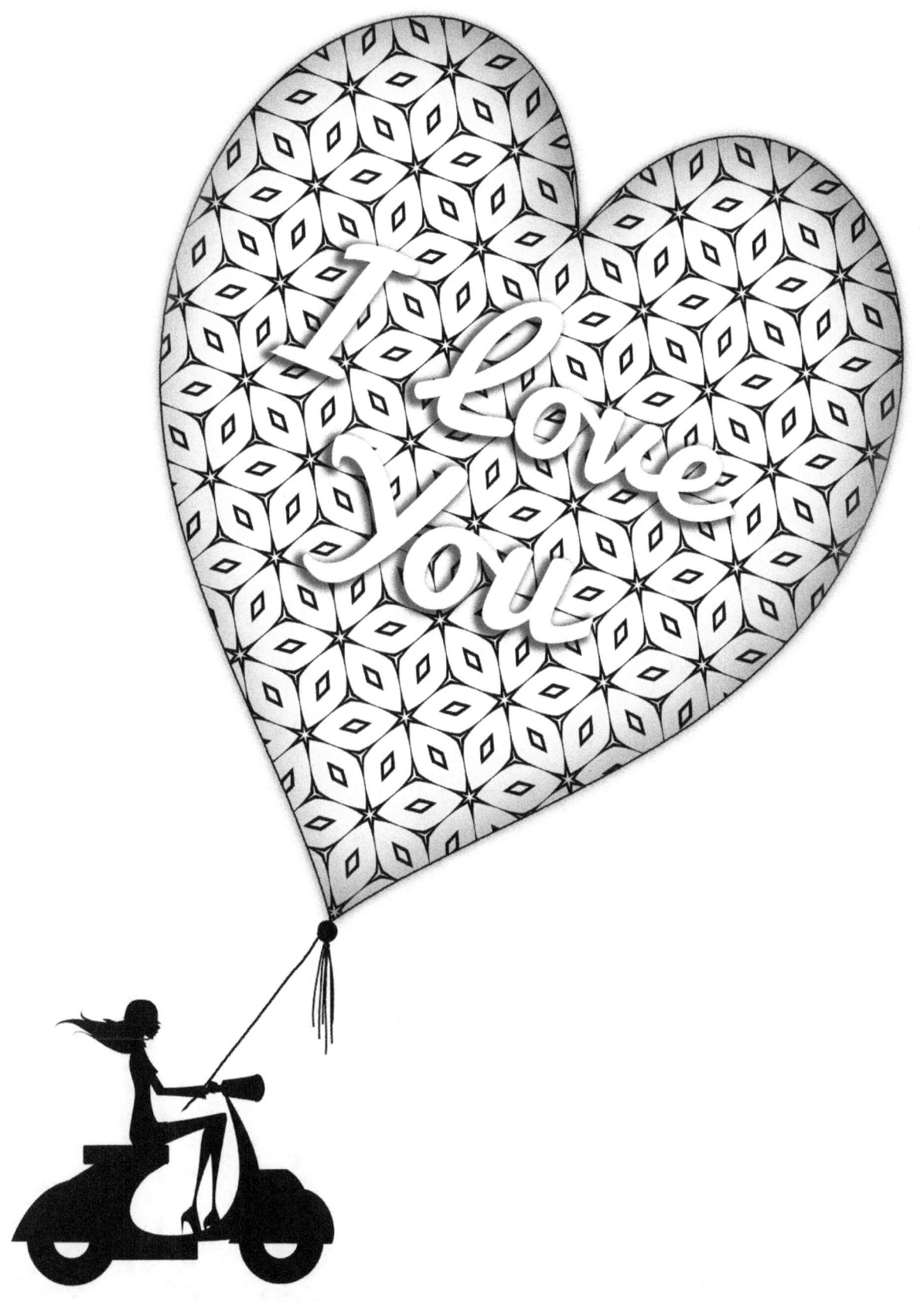

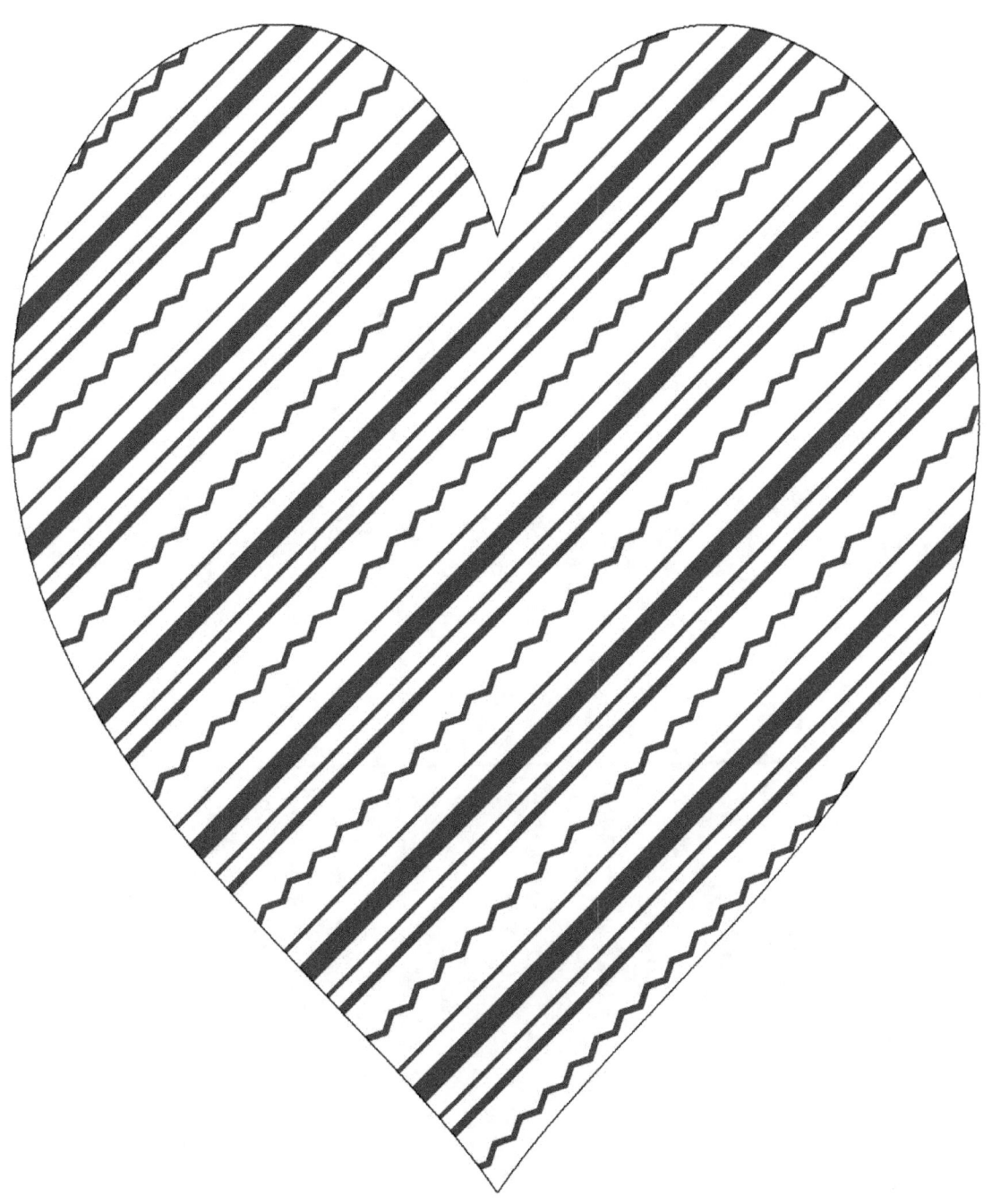

Corner Heart
Bookmarks

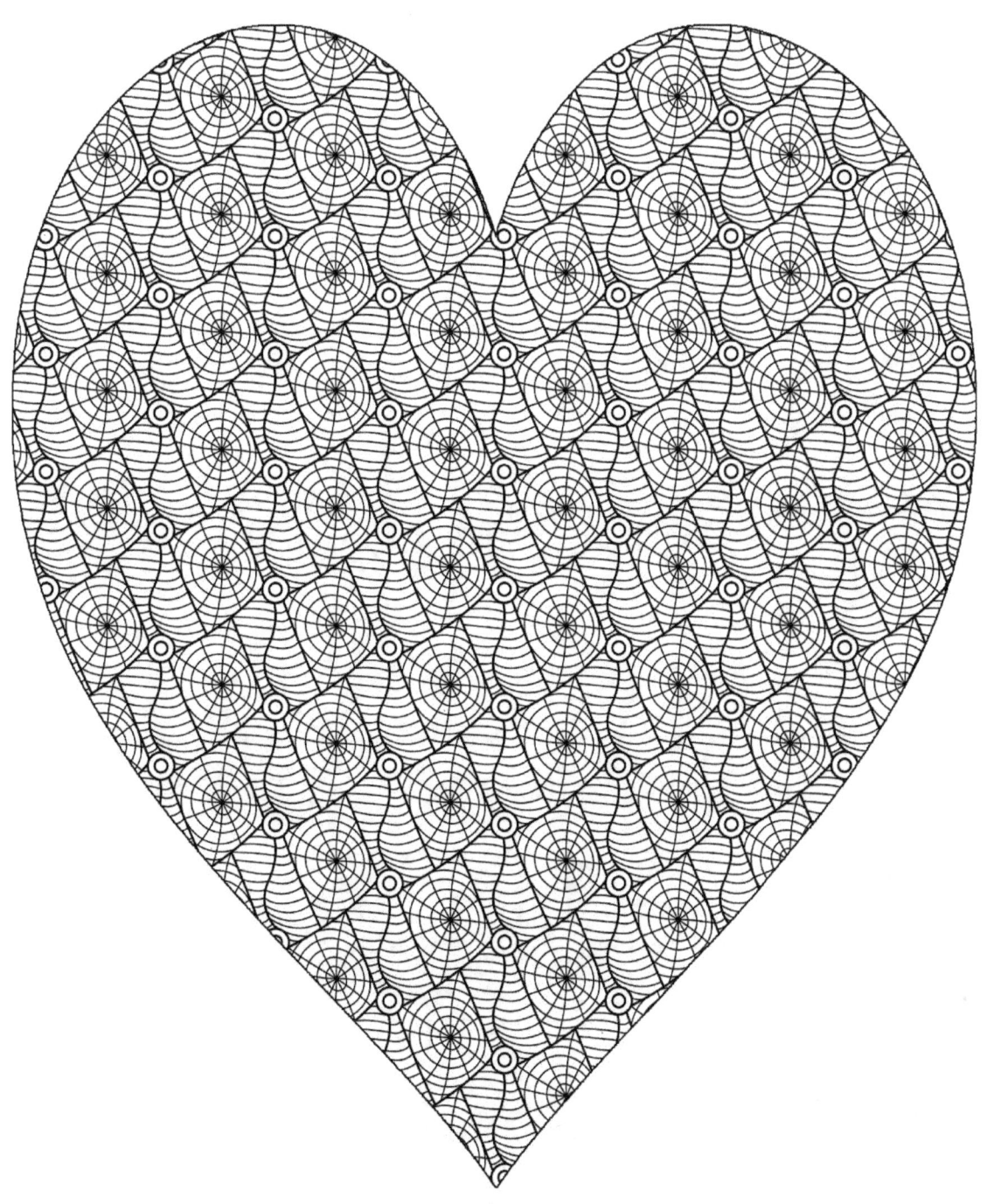

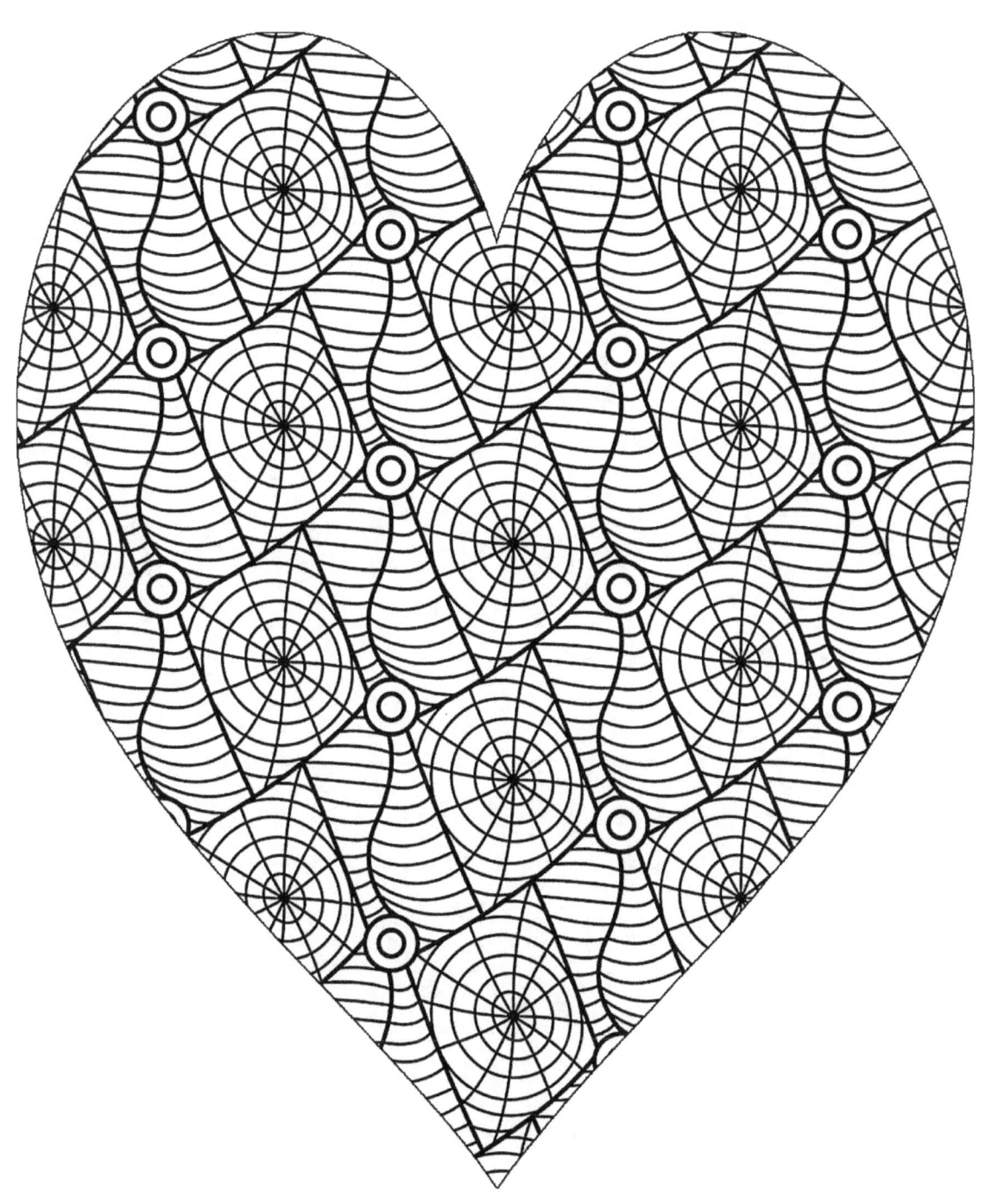

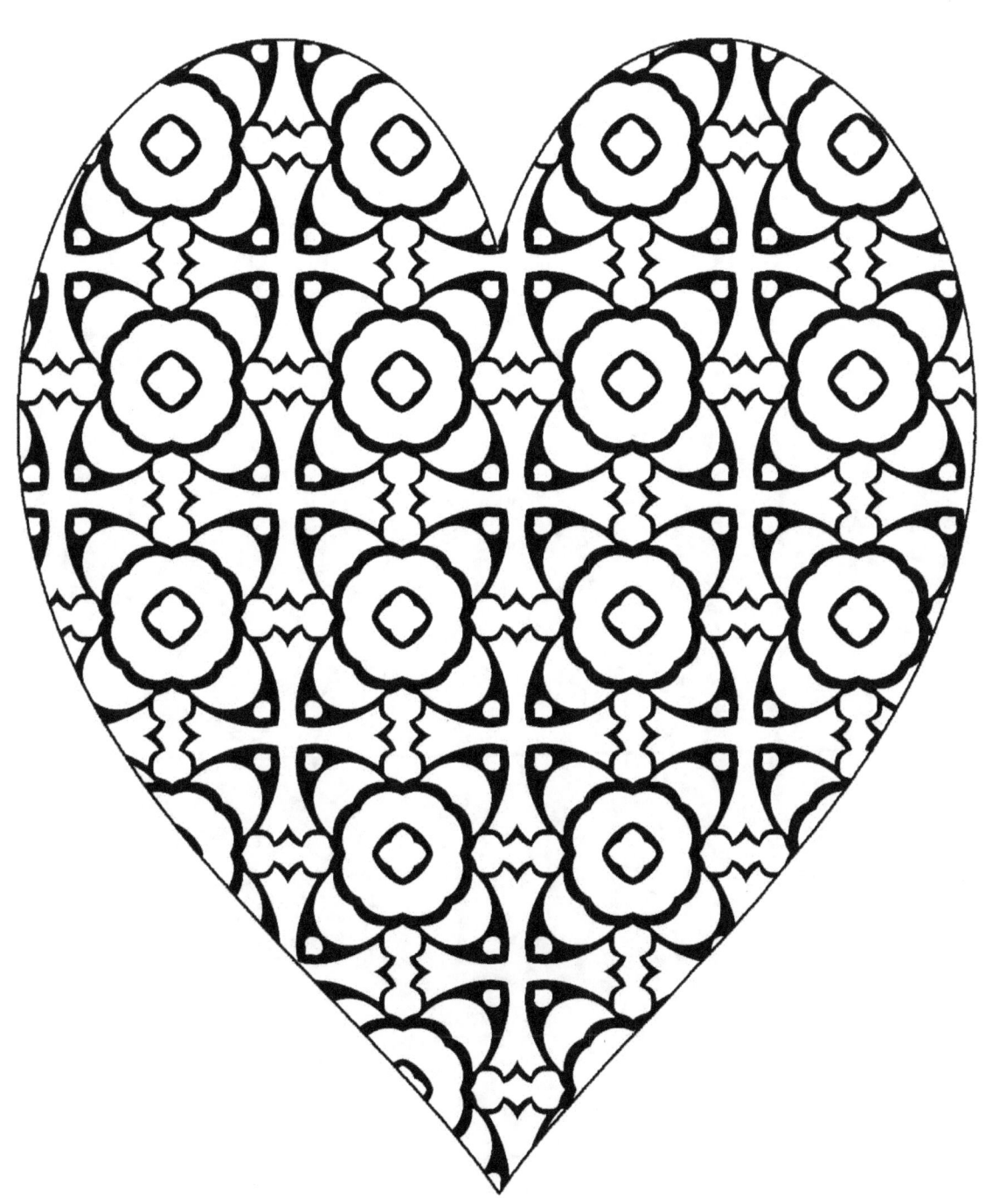

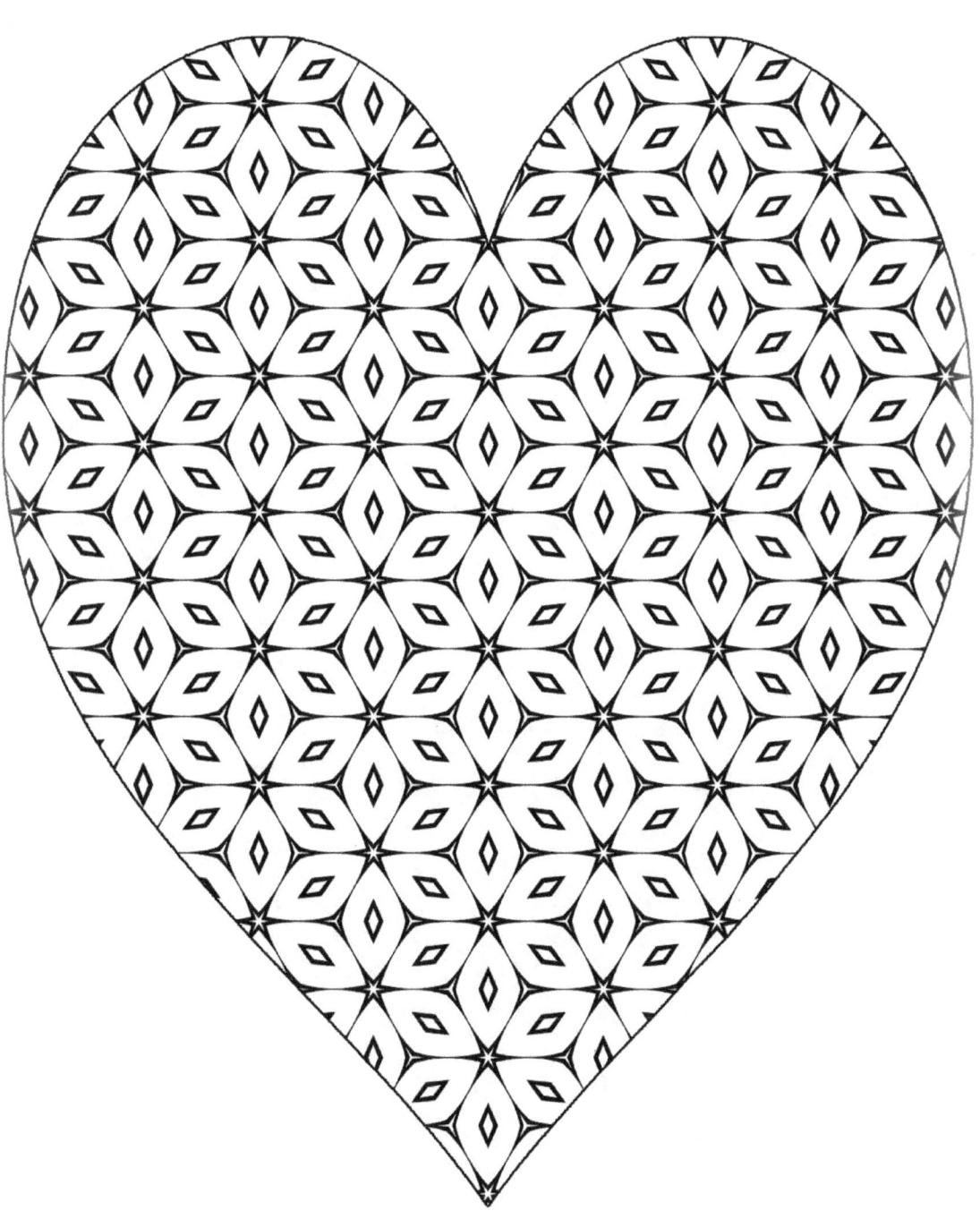

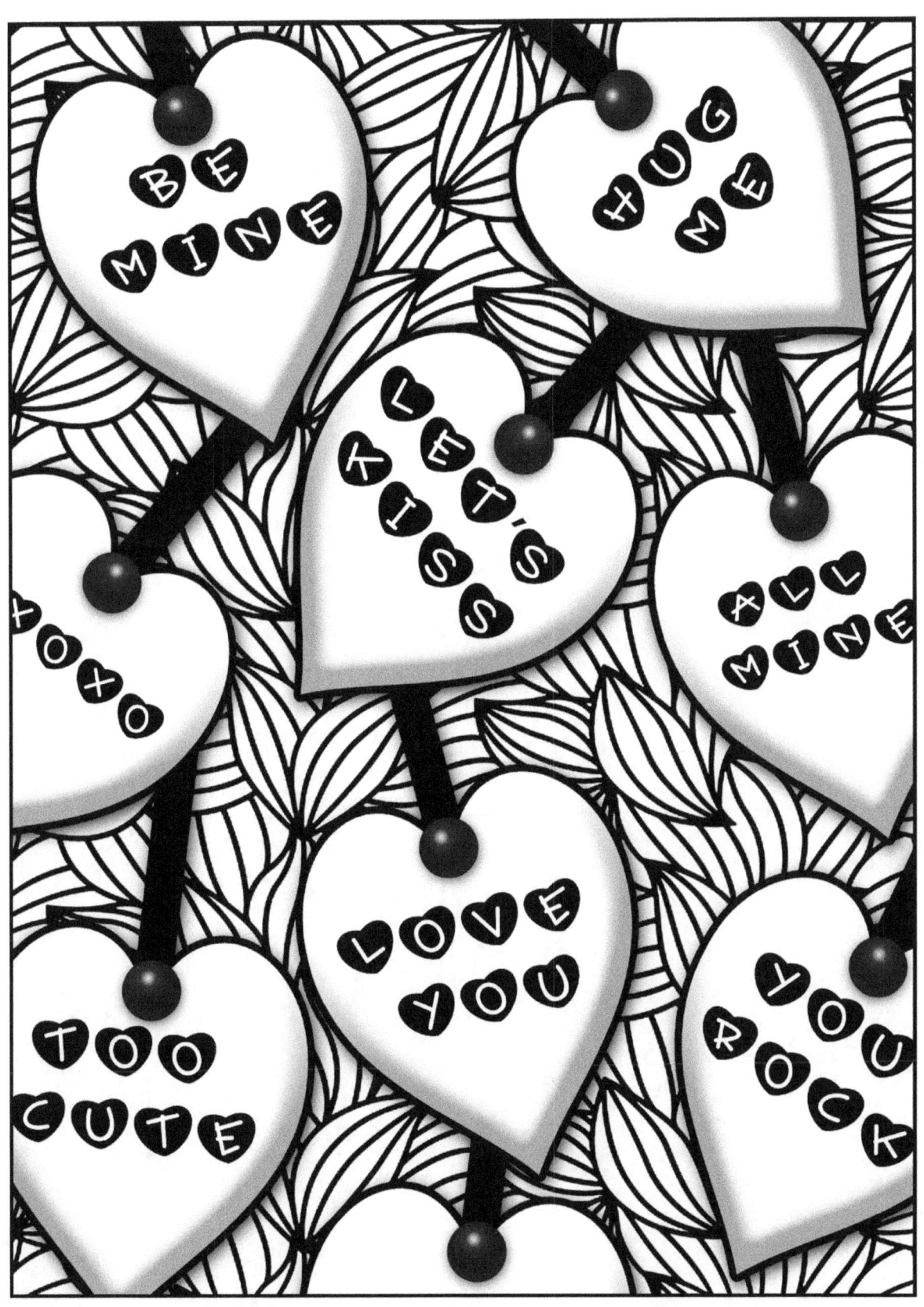

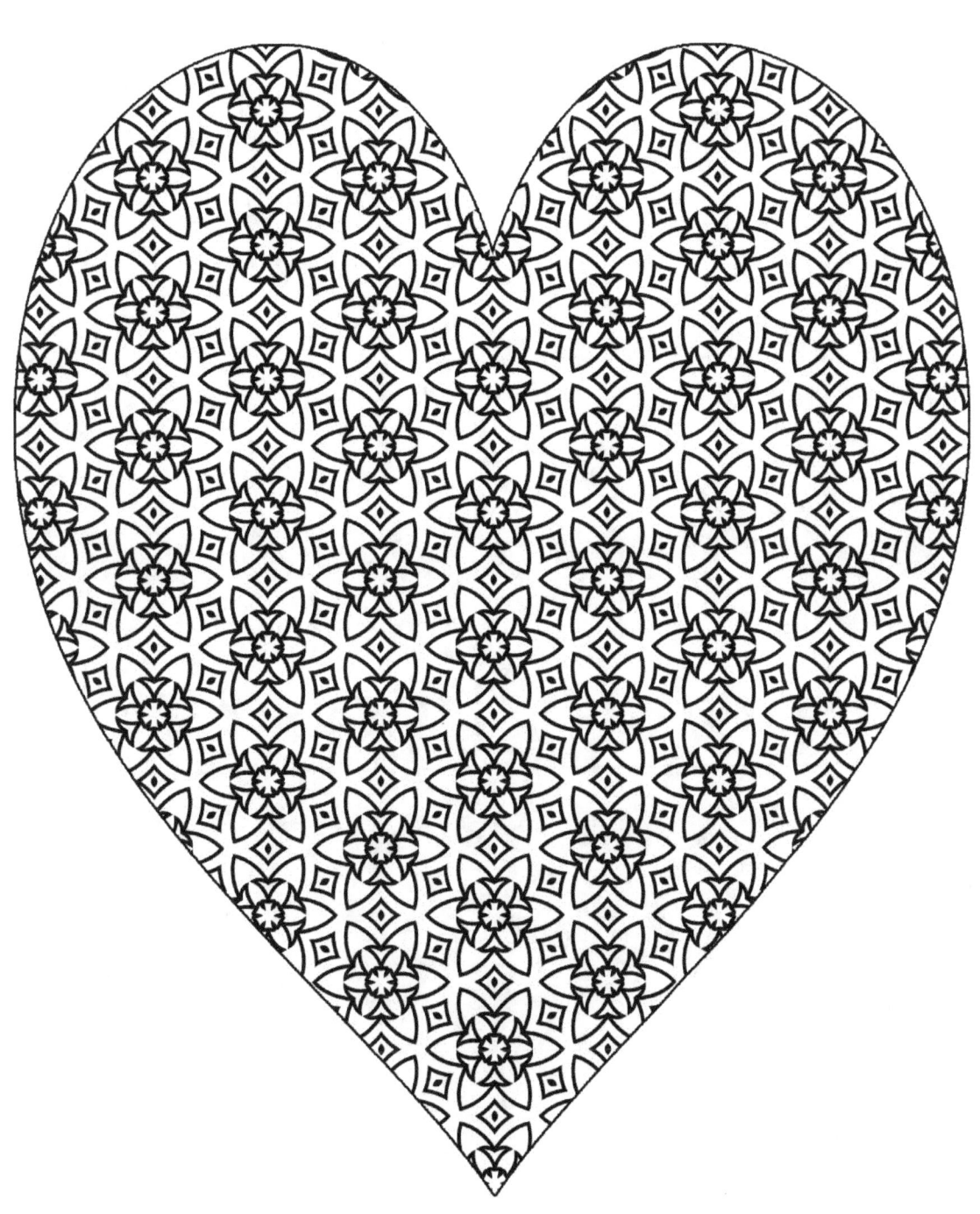

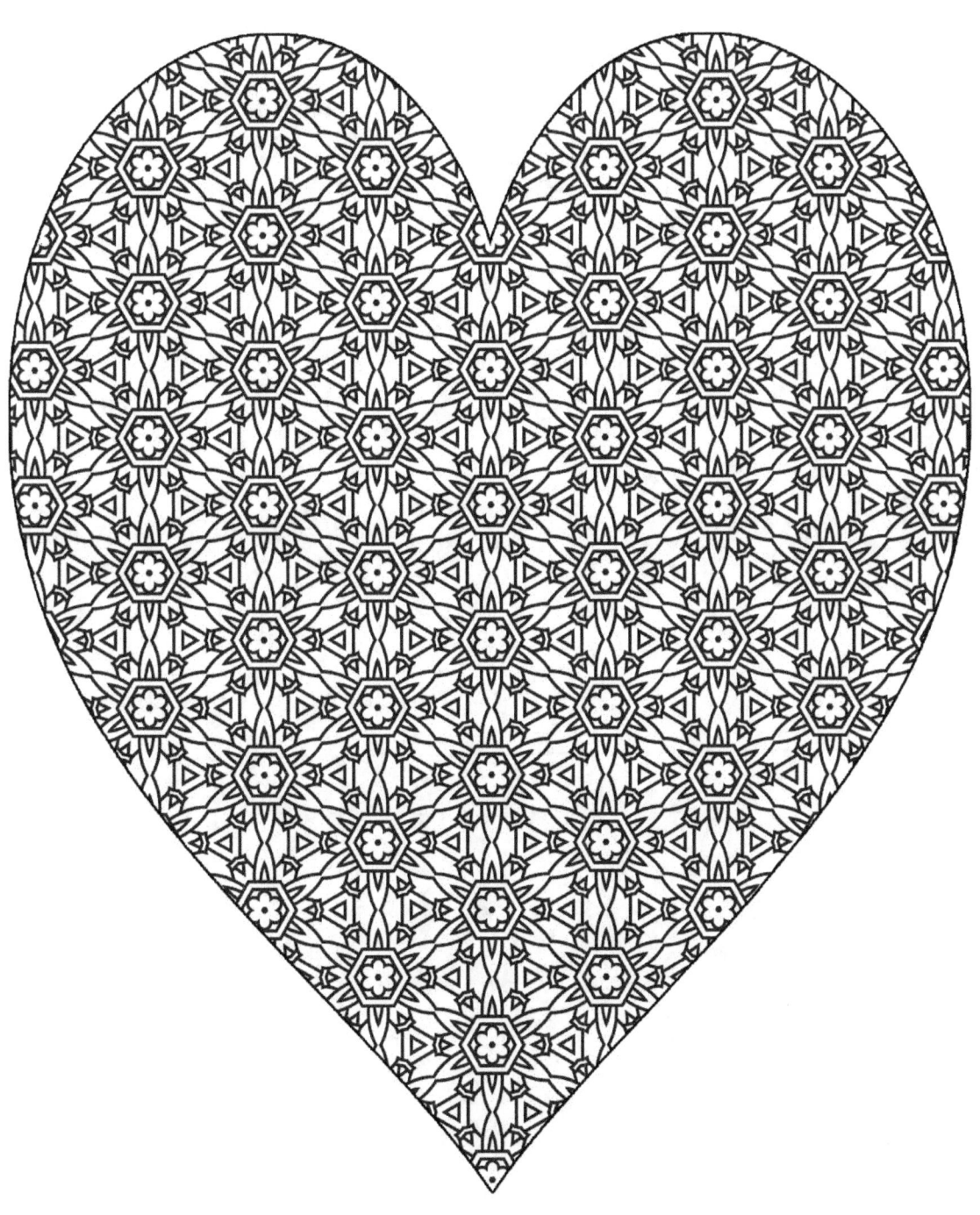

Corner Heart
Bookmarks

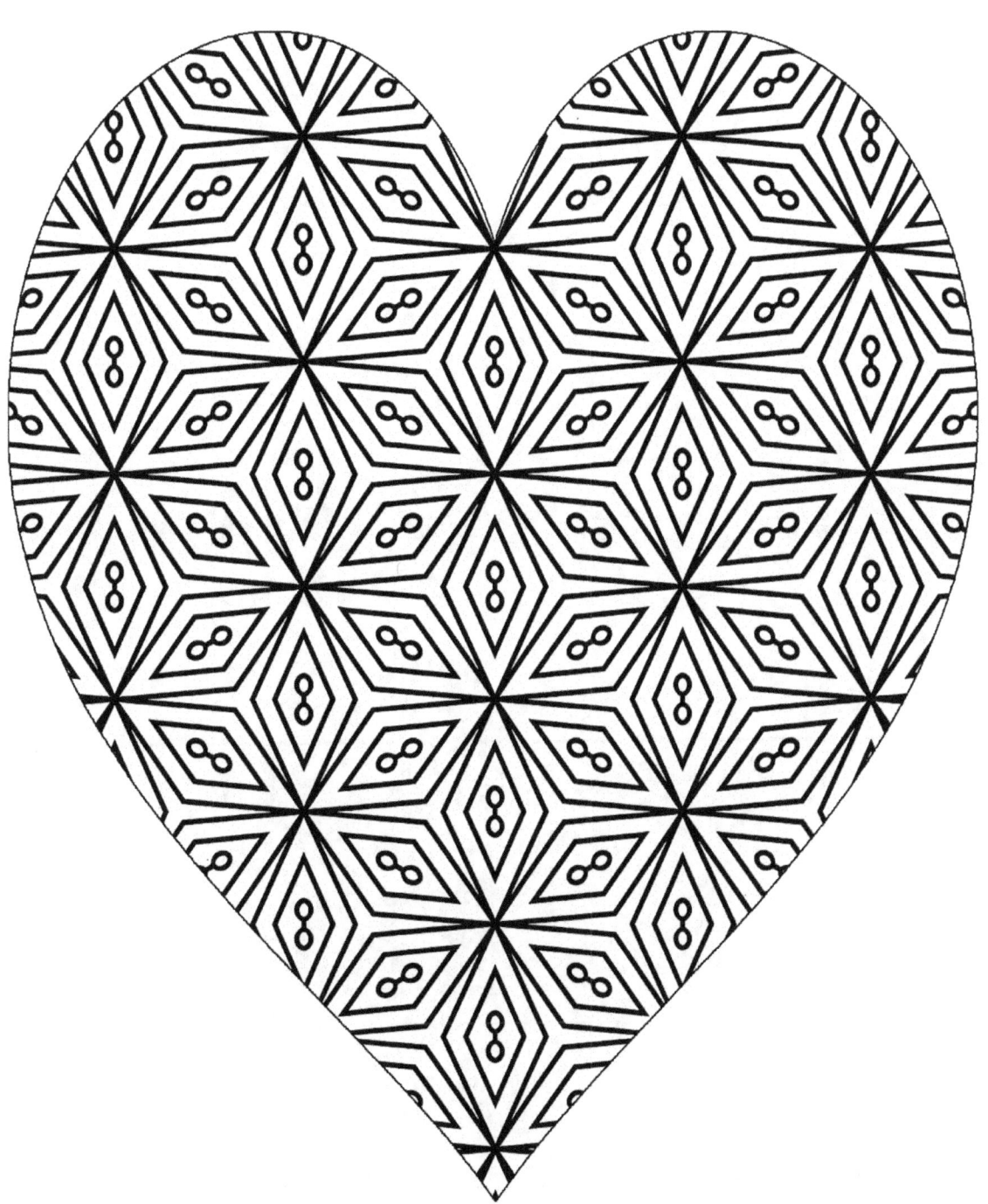

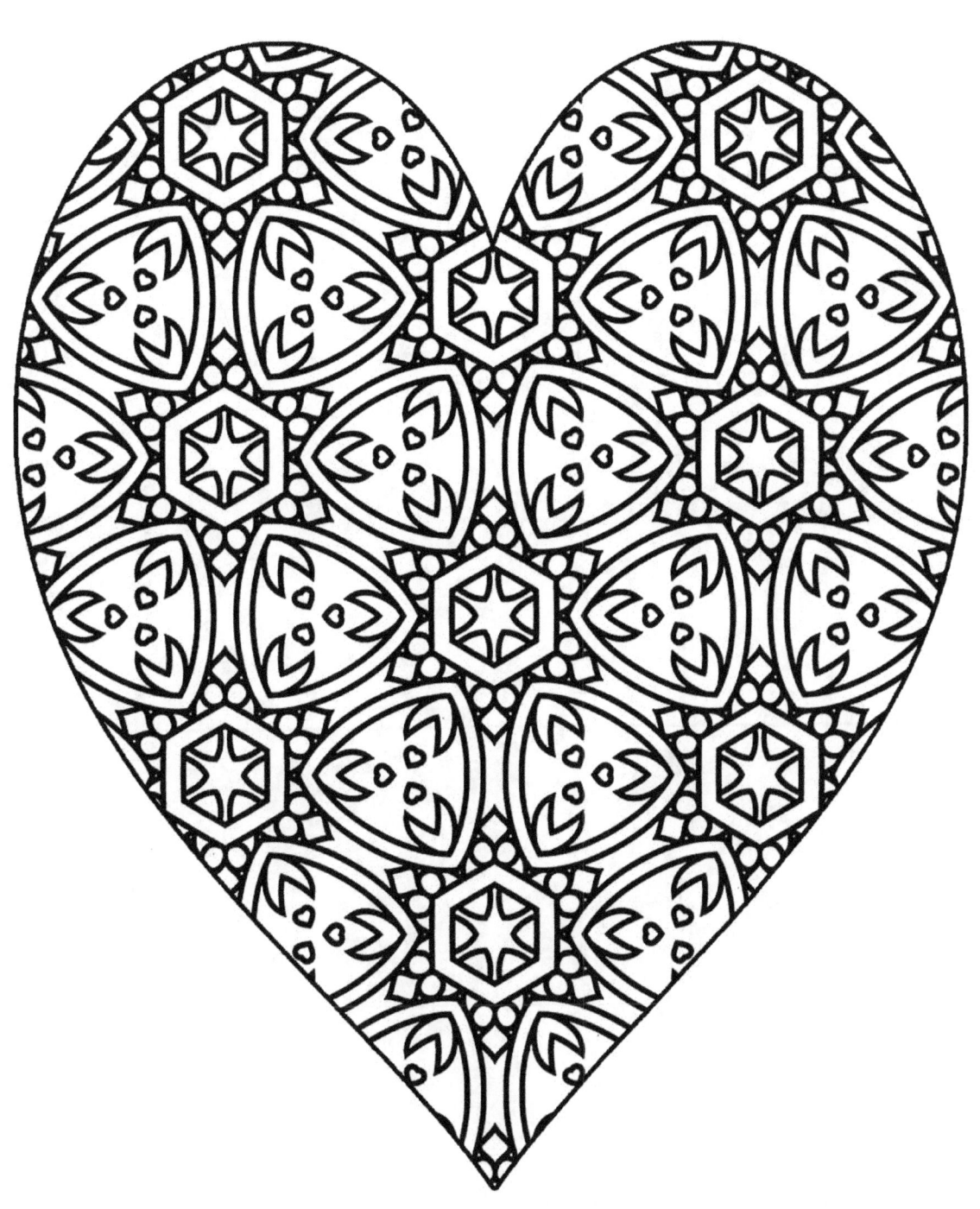

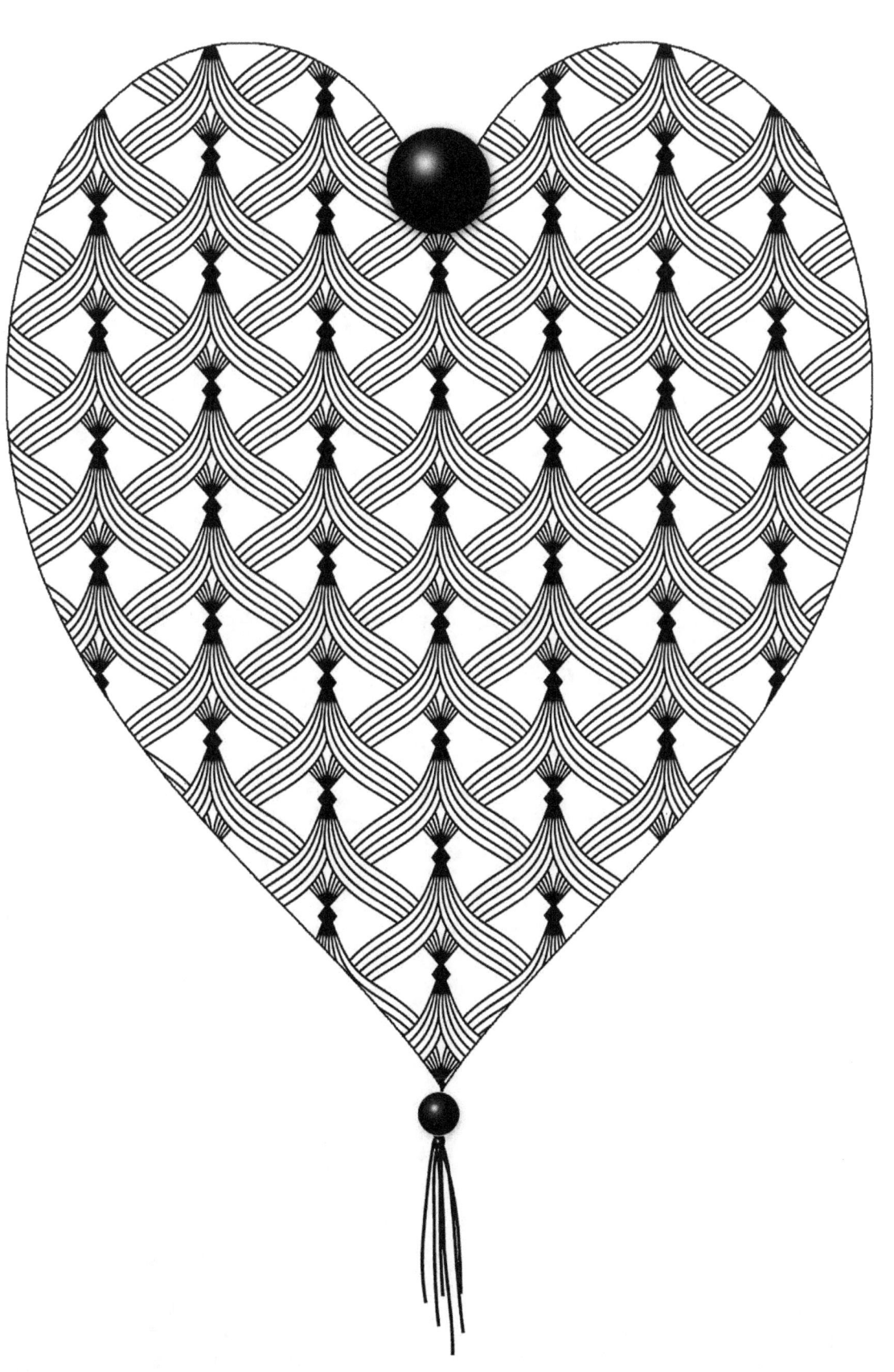

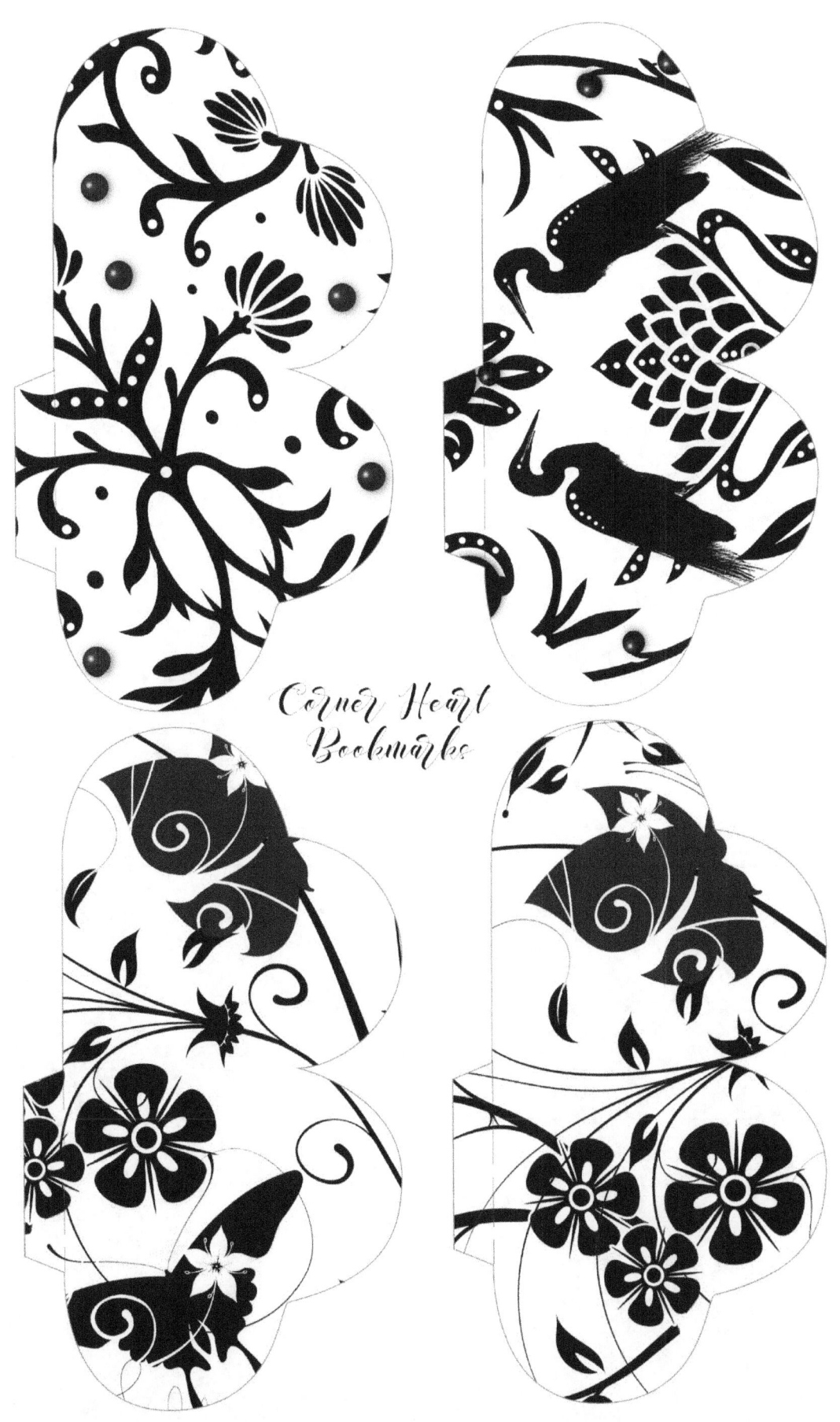

Corner Heart
Bookmarks

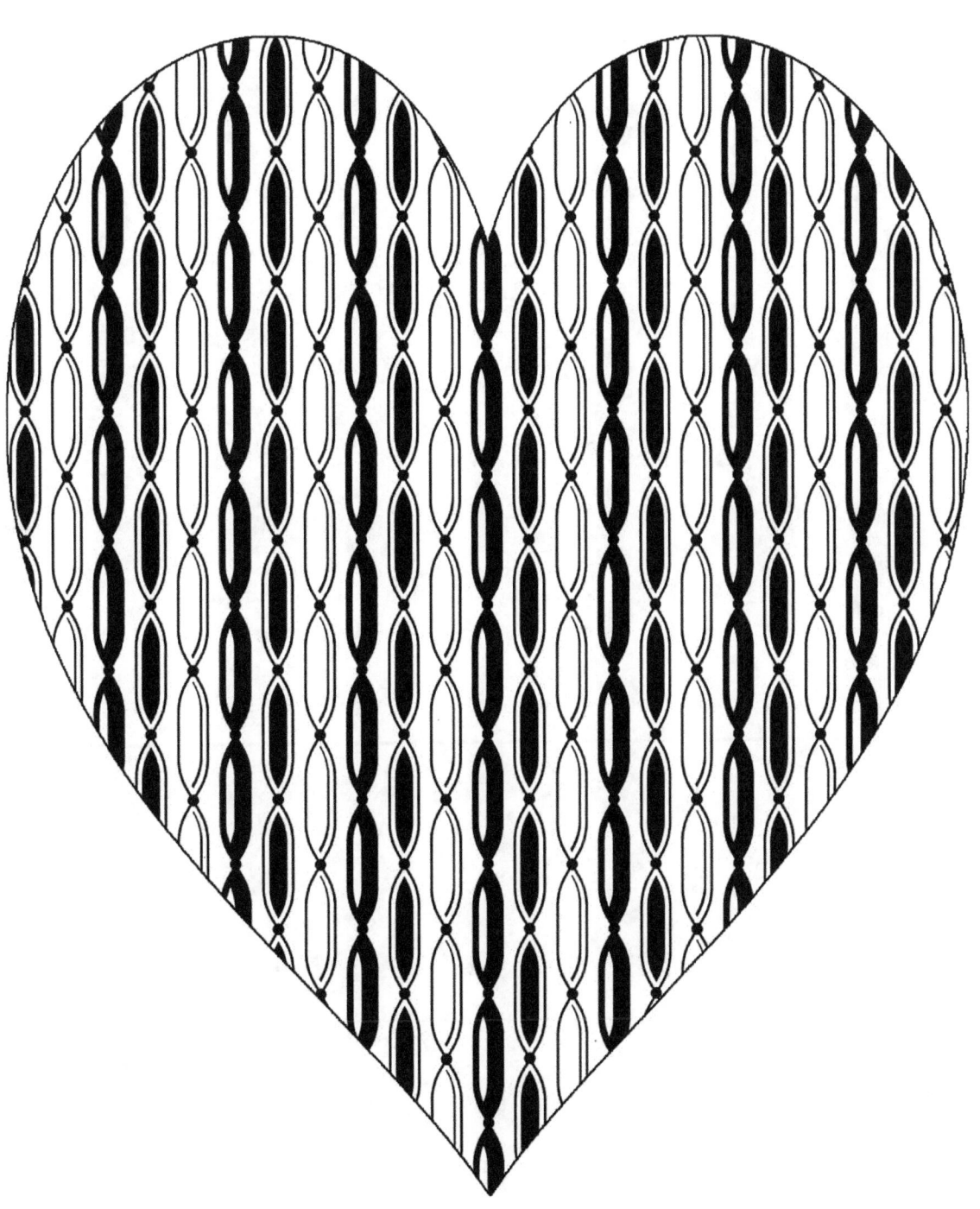

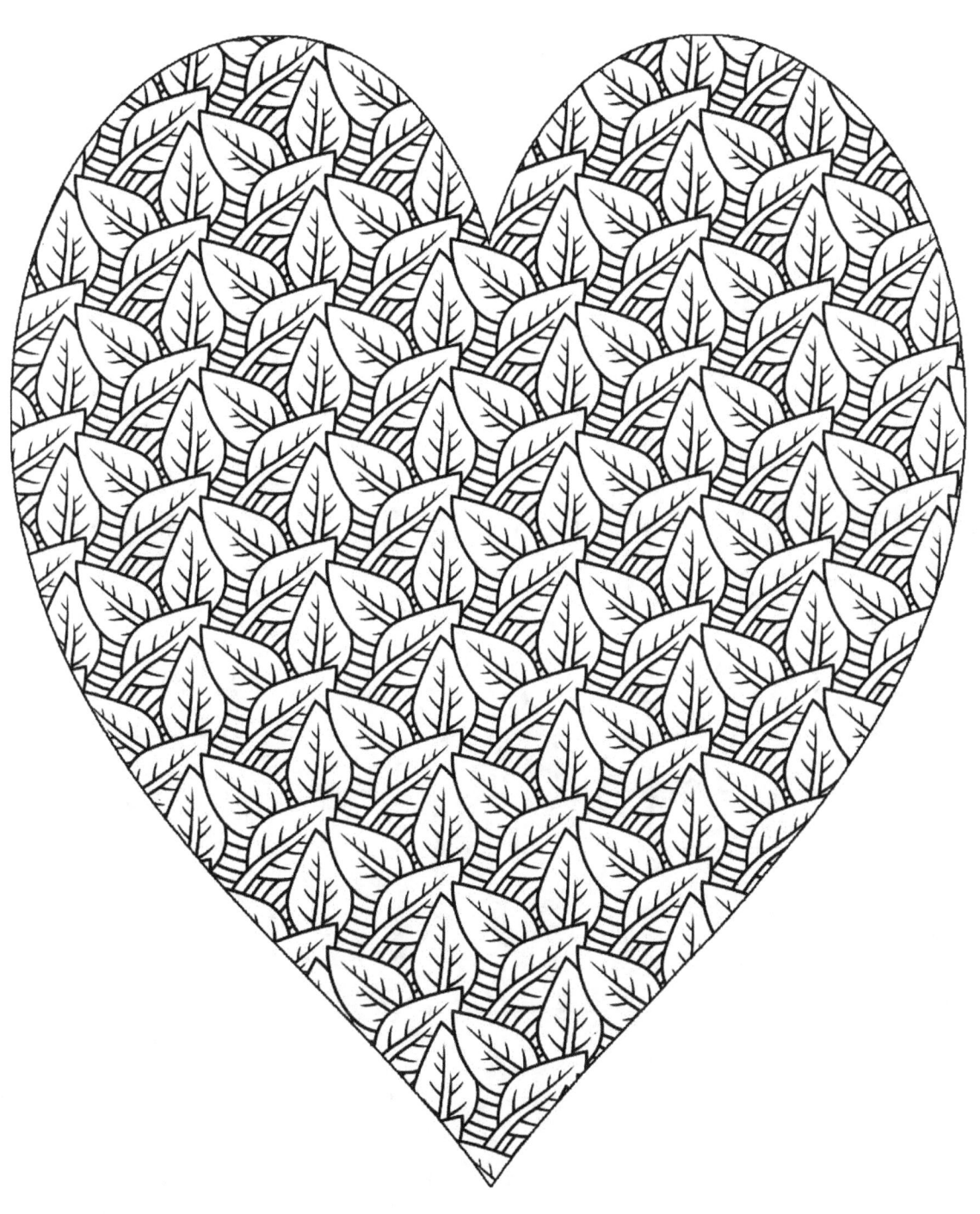

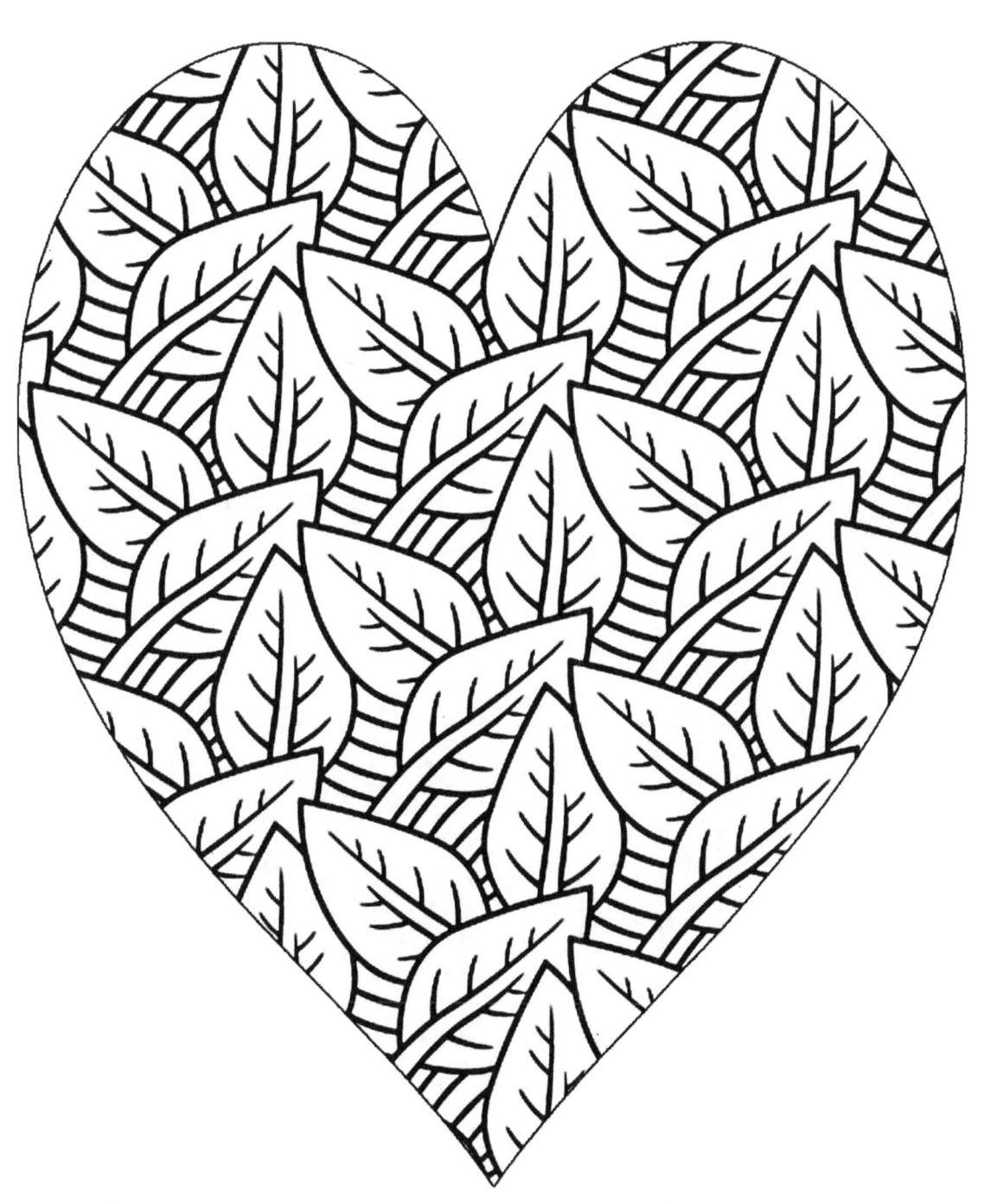

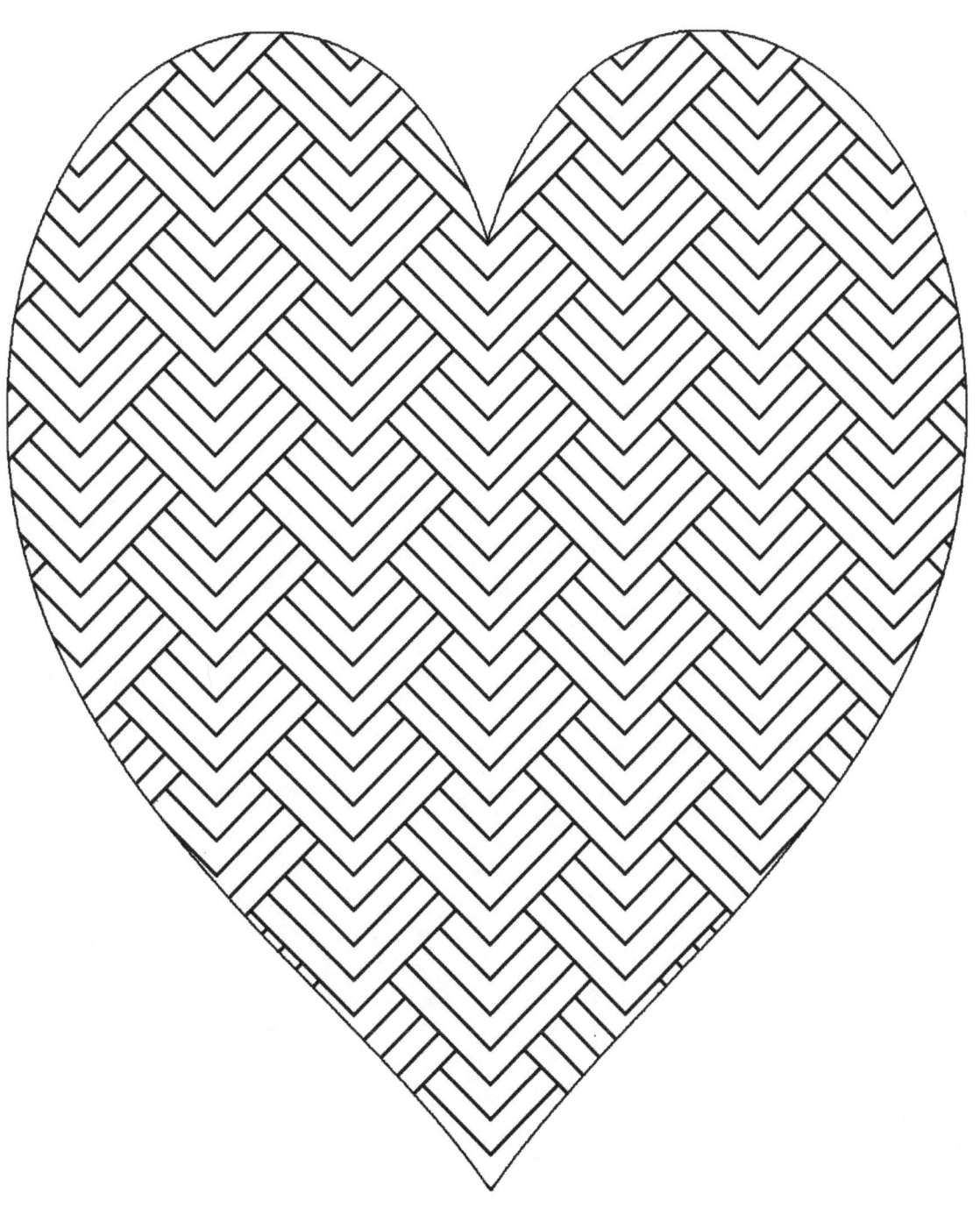

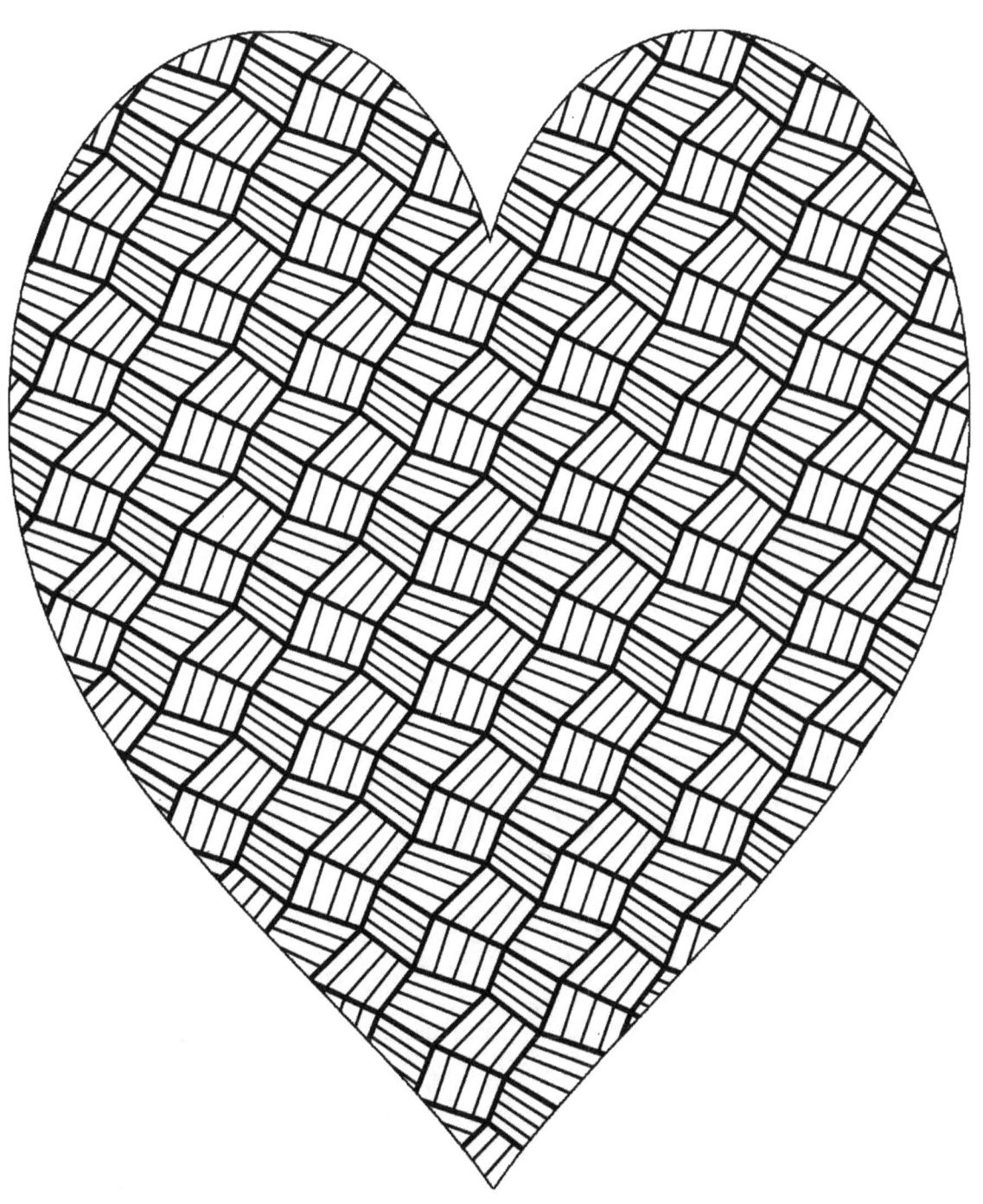

Inked Hearts Tags

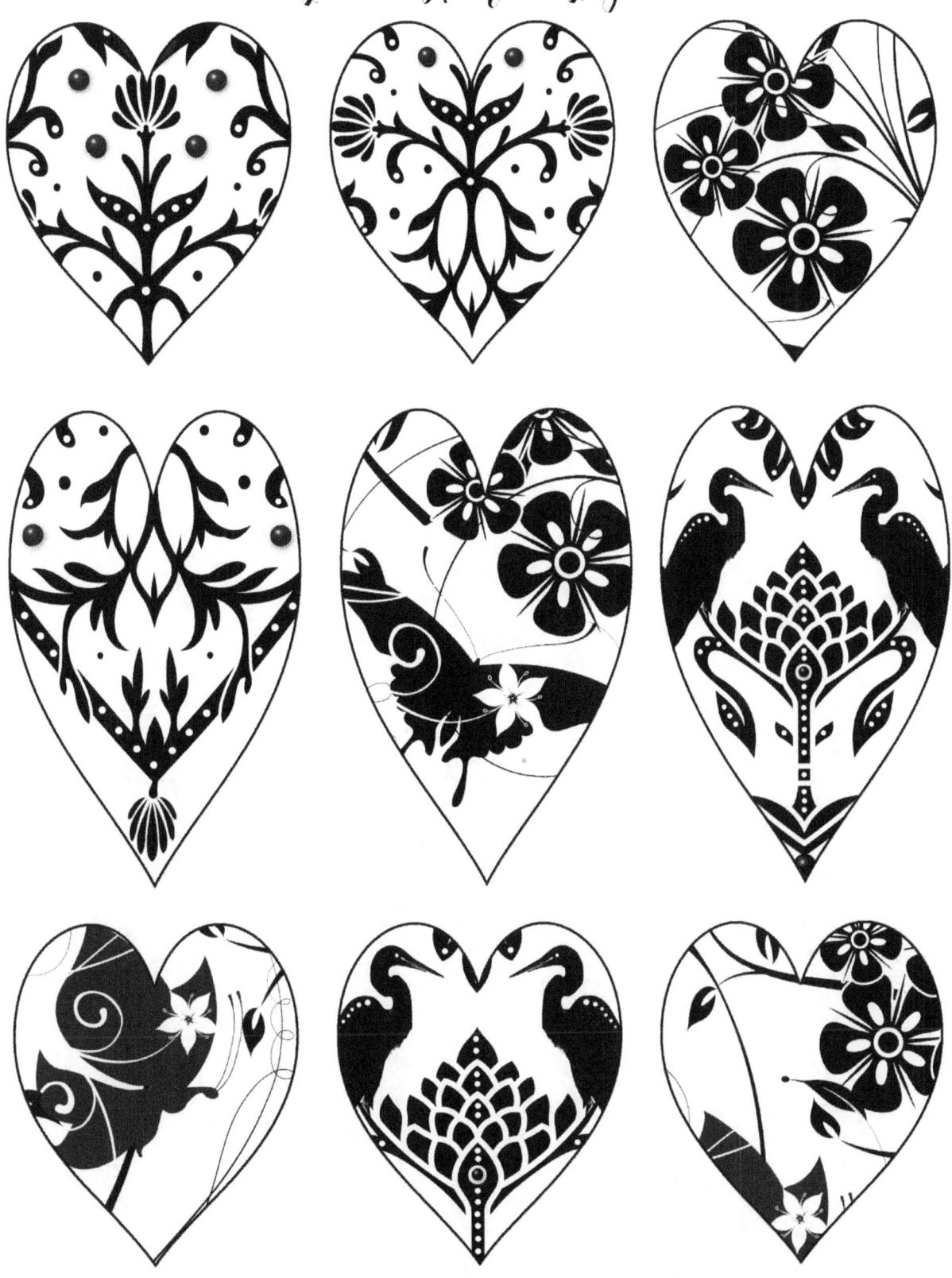

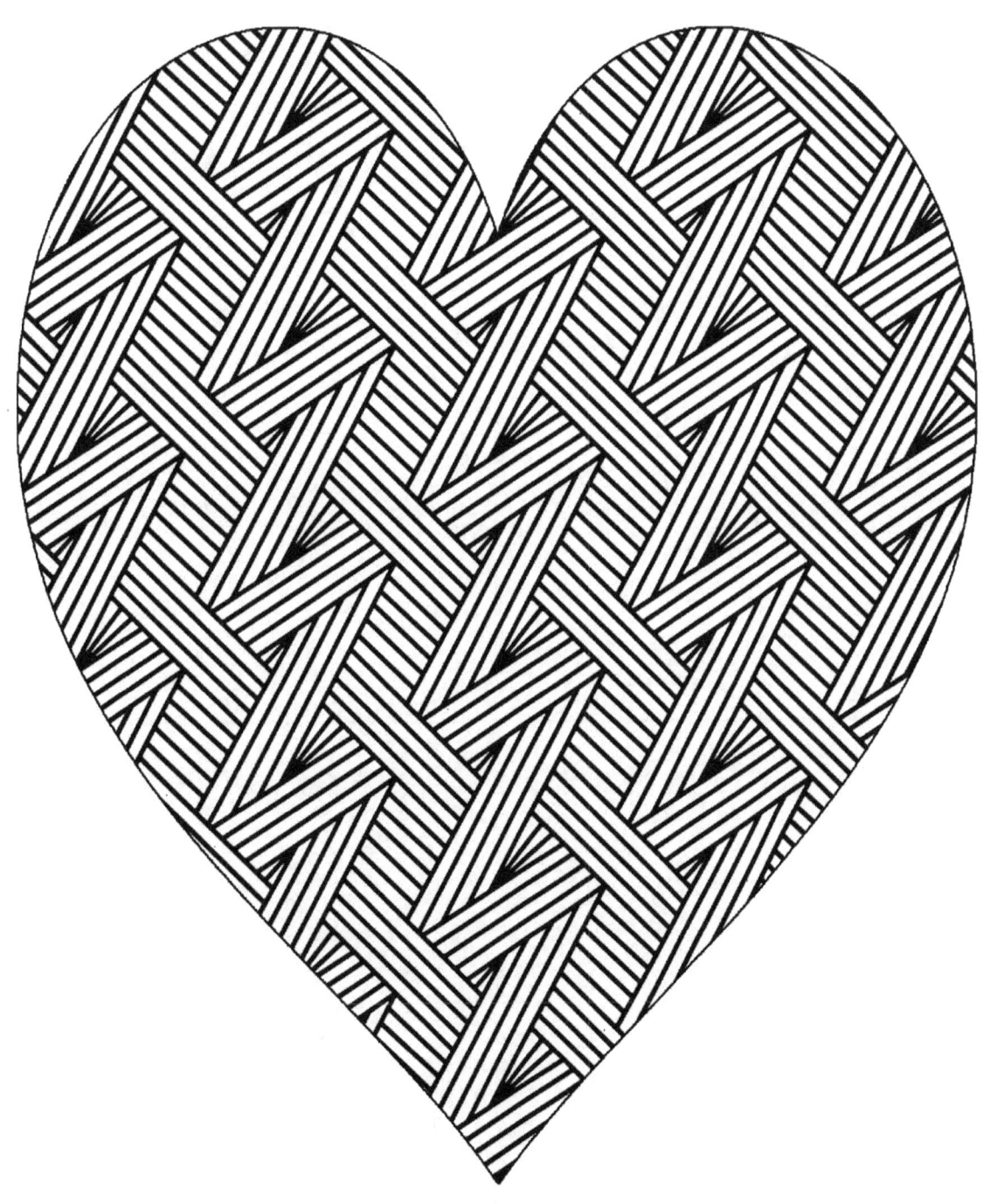

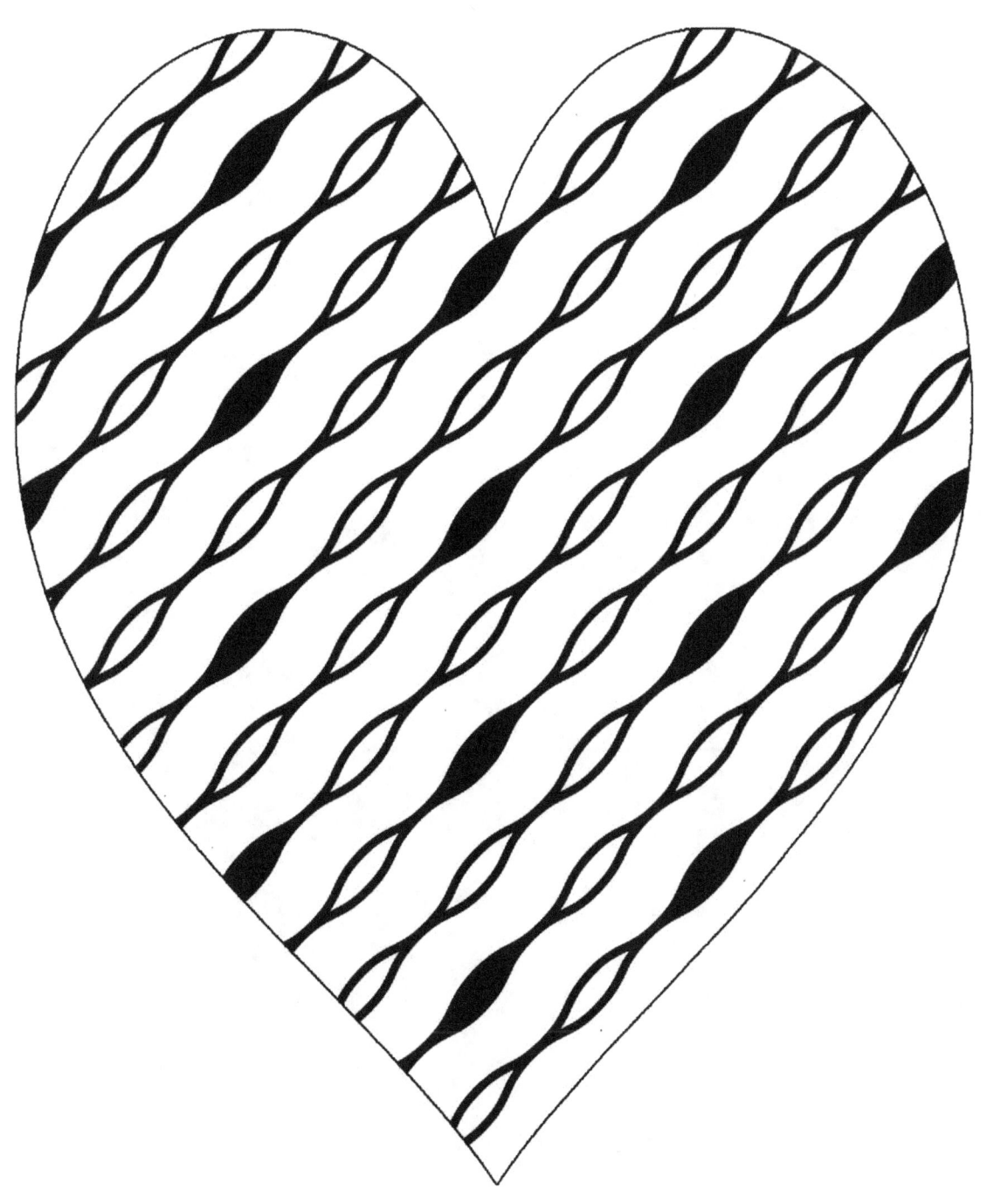

Have you seen my other Books on Amazon?

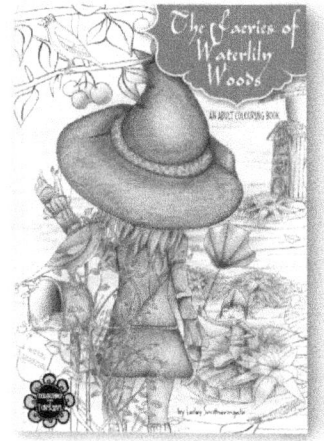

The Faeries of Waterlily Woods
Adult Colouring Book
- Line art Edition

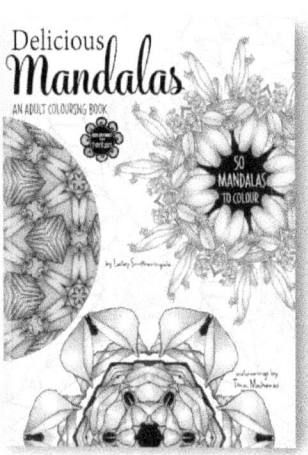

Delicious Mandalas
Adult Colouring Book

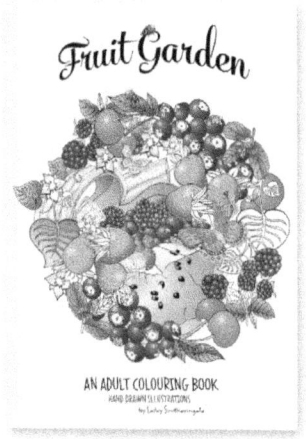

Fruit Garden
Adult Colouring Book

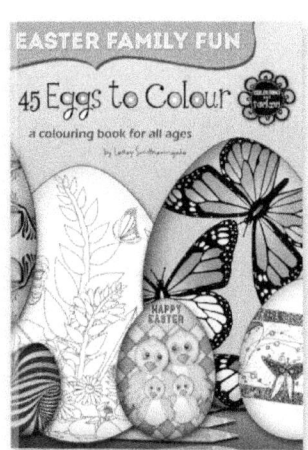

45 Eggs to Colour -
Easter Family Fun
Colouring Book for all Ages

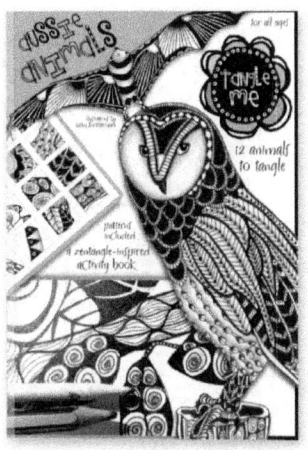

Tangle Me Aussie Animals -
a Zentangle-inspired
Activity Book for all Ages

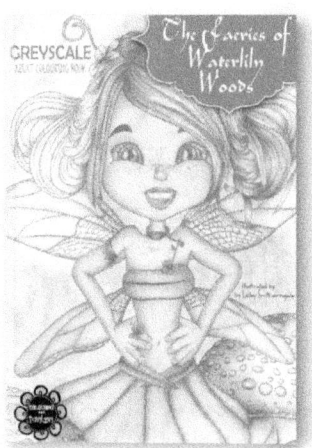

The Faeries of Waterlily Woods
Adult Colouring Book
- Greyscale Edition

See them all on my Author Page on Amazon at
https://www.amazon.com/author/lesleysmitheringale

www.ingramcontent.com/pod-product-compliance
Lightning Source LLC
Chambersburg PA
CBHW080300180526
45167CB00006B/2610